Analysis of Enforcement of Intellectual Property Rights Related to Standard Technology in East Asia and Europe

JN034586

近代科学社 Digital

Preface

The author sincerely dedicates this book to my dear mentors, Prof. Ariel Ezrachi, Prof. Graeme Dinwoodie and Prof. Dev Gangjee at The University of Oxford, Prof. Sir Robin Jacob at University College London, and Dr. Ariannna Andregianni at The University of Edinburgh, along with Prof. Jacques de Werra at The University of Geneva, Mr. Ignacio de Castro at WIPO Arbitration and Mediation Center, scholar and lawyer friends in the UK, Switzerland WIPO/WTO and Japan, and my loving wife and daughter, who kindly keep supporting my research.

February 2021

Seiya S. Takeuchi

Table of Contents

Chapter 3 Restriction of IP Enforcement : Situation in Europe

Chapter 4 SEP Enforcement : Samsung's SEP Cases in Japan and Europe

Chapter 5 SEP enforcement : Implication of Samsung's SEP Cases for East Asia

Chapter 6 Conclusion : 'Regulatory Competition' situation in East Asia

APPENDIX A   JFTC IP Guideline

APPENDIX B   JPO SEP License Negotiation Rules

Chapter 1

Introduction :
Influence of the European
Legal Analysis to
East Asian Countries

In response to the increase of disputes on enforcement of intellectual property rights (hereinafter 'IP rights') related to standard technology in the global market, the governments of Japan, Korea and China have been intensively working on new guidelines and reformation of their law system since 2014. More concretely, following the European Commission's decision in the case of Samsung Electronics's enforcement of standard essential patents (hereinafter 'SEP') in 2014 and the European Court of Justice's judgement in Huawei vs. ZTE case in 2015, the authorities in those East Asian countries incorporated the European approach into their legal framework of restriction on enforcement of the IP rights incorporated in standard technology.

Firstly, in Japan, the IP High Courtprovided its judgement on Samsung's SEP enforcement in 2014, and the Japan Fair Trade Commission revised its guideline for the restriction on SEP enforcement in 2016. Furthermore, the Japan Patent Office has provided its new guidance for the negotiations of SEP licenses in 2018.

Also, the Korean Fair Trade Commission revised its guideline for the restriction on enforcement of IP rights incorporated in standard technology in 2014. In response to some concerns to the revised guideline by the industry, the guideline was revised again in 2016. In addition, the Patents Law of Korea has newly employed the punitive damages system in 2019.

Furthermore, the authorities in China, the State Administration for Industry and Commerce of the People's Republic of China (SAIC), the National Development and Reform Commission (NDRC) and Anti-Monopoly Commission (AMC), have been announcing multiple guidelines for restrictions on enforcement of the IP rights incorporated in standard technology. However, those guidelines are trying to incorporate an approach similar to the European Essential Facilitiesdoctrine with unique interpretations, and the concerns of possible restraint of technological innovation and incentive of technology development have been expressed by the industry.

This book will explain the recent policy-making situation of the aforementioned East Asian countries and within Europe and introduce the author's analysis of the 'Regulatory Competition' situation., i.e., the situation where multiple countries compete with each other for more aggressive regulation policies in East Asia.

Chapter 2

IP Enforcement : Situation of Japan

1   Introduction

This chapter will introduce the traditional legal approach under the Japanese Anti-Monopoly Act (hereinafter 'AMA') of restriction on the refusal of license for IP rights incorporated in standard technology.

The refusal of license for IP rights incorporated in standard technology could cause a restraint of market competition when the refusing party holds the dominant position in the market. Although AMA's intervention in refusal of license is required for recovering market competition, we should pay careful attention to the negative influence caused by the AMA's intervention to the innovation in the industry and the incentive to develop technology.

On the other hand, we should note that the AMA of Japan has its unique Unfair Trade Practicesregulation framework which may allow the Japanese authority its excessive intervention in the field of IP rights enforcement. A careful assessment of the criteria of AMA's intervention in refusal of license for IP rights is important for maintaining a balance between the protection of market competition and the promotion of innovation and technology development.

In order to clarify the criteria of AMA's intervention in refusal of license for IP rights incorporated in standard technology, this chapter will explain its typical situations, i.e., the Insider situation, the Outsider situation and the Ambush situation, along with their anti-competitive effect in the market. Then, this chapter will examine the criteria of AMA's regulation policy on those situations through an analysis of decisions by the court and the Japan Fair Trade Commission (hereinafter 'JFTC').

The refusal of license for IP rights incorporated in standard technology can be categorized into three situations, i.e., Insider situation, Outsider situation or Ambush situation. The Insider situation and the Outsider situation are mainly discussed in relation with the IP rights incorporated in the de-jure standard technology which involves a formulated standardized process in standard setting organizations (hereinafter 'SSO') or forum activities. On the other hand, the Ambush case is normally considered in relation to the IP rights incorporated in the de-facto standard which is formed through competition in the market[1].

1.See Japan Fair Trade Commission, *Guidelines for the Use of Intellectual Property under the Antimonopoly Act*, 28 Sep. 2007, Section 3-1 & 4-2 [hereinafter *JFTC IP Guideline*].

2 The Typical Situations

2-1 Insider Situation and Outsider Situation

The Insider situation can be typically found in the standard setting situation as follows: a) SSOis established by the entities holding the patents which are essential for use of the standard technology (hereinafter 'standard essential patent' or 'SEP'), b) those entities search and declare the existence of their SEP as members of the SSO, and c) the grant of license for their SEP under the fair, reasonable and non-discriminatory terms (hereinafter 'FRANDterms') will be obliged to the entities.

However, there exists a possibility that some entities holding SEP may offer a license with unreasonable terms, such as excessively high amount of royalty, against their license obligation under the FRAND terms. In this case those entities' conduct is against their commitment to the FRAND license and this will be regarded as abusive enforcement of the patent in the Insider situation.

On the other hand, the Outsider situation can be realized through the standard setting situation as follows: a) SSOis established by the entities holding SEP, b) however, some other entities holding SEP choose not to become members of the SSO and conceal the existence of their SEP, and c) those non-member entities will enforce their SEP to users of standard technology set by the SSO after waiting for the widespread adoption of the standard technology in the market. In this case, the non-member entities' enforcement of SEP to users of the standard technology would be regarded as abusive enforcement of the patents in the Outsider situation.

Also, we should note, in the Outsider situation, the non-member entity could indirectly use its influence and make its patents employed as SEP. For example, some member entities of SSOcan be manipulated by the non-member entity to induce specifications of standard technology to incorporate non-member entity's patents.

2-2 Ambush Situation

The Ambush situation can be found in the following forming process of the de-facto standard technology: a) one technical specification becomes widespread technology, i.e., de-facto standard technology, used by a majority of users through competition in the market, b) an entity holding the patents incorporated in the de-facto standard technology will wait for further spread of the standard technology until the users are locked into the standard technology, c) the patents holder then enforce its patents against users of the standard technology for pursuing excessive benefit from the patents. In this case, enforcement of those patents by such an entity can be regarded as abusive enforcement of patents in the Ambush situation.

As introduced in the above, the typical situations of refusal to license can be categorized into three situations in accordance with the characteristics of the standard setting process. The next section will explain the anti-competition aspect of each situation.

3   Anti-Competitive Effect Caused by IP Rights Enforcement Against the Use of Standard Technology

The anti-competitive effects caused by the refusal to license in the Insider situation, the Outsider situation or the Ambush situation can be triggered as follows. It should be noted on the analysis of each situation that the Insider situation may involve any arbitrary conduct, such as a commitment of FRANDlicense in the standardization process, although the Outsider situation or the Ambush situation does not normally involve such an arbitrary conduct.

3-1   Uniqueness of the IP Rights Enforcement Related to Standard Technology

In the Insider situation or the Outsider situation, the users of the de-jure standard technology normally rely upon the SEP holder's commitment for a grant of license under the FRANDterms. As a result, if the SEP holder refuses to grant a license for SEP, those users have to give up their business or products or services incorporating the standard technology. This means that the users will not be able to recover their investment through the revenue from their business in the market. Under this users' lock-in situation, those users will have no choice but to accept the SEP holders' offer of abusive license terms which is not in compliance with the FRAND terms. Therefore, the abusive license terms can be forced on the users by the SEP holder's arbitrary conduct[2].

In the Ambush situation, the enforcement of patent incorporated in standard technology can bring the patent holder a superior bargaining position because of the user's lock-in to the de-facto standard technology, and result in an excessive income from the patent. More precisely, the users of a widespread standard technology in the market can be locked-in to products or services incorporating the standard technology due to the

---

2.Shapiro & Varian, Information Rules: A Strategic Guide to the Network Economy 175-179 (1998), Greenhalgh & Rogers, Innovation, Intellectual Property and Economic Growth 184-186 (2010) [hereinafter *Greenhalgh & Rogers*], Carrier, Standard Setting Analysis Under US Law, Intellectual Property and Competition Law: New Frontiers 359-361 (Steven Anderman & Ariel Ezrachi eds., 2011), Takigawa, High-tech sangyou no chitekizaisanken to dokukinhou [IP rights in High-tech industry and Anti-monopoly Act] 162-166 (2000) [hereinafter *Takigawa2000*].

network effects existing among those users.

Under this situation, if the patent holder enforces its patent upon those users after deliberately waiting for a dissemination of products or services knowing the users will become locked-in due to the existence of the network effects, and later requires a payment of excessively high amounts of royalty, those users will have no choice but to accept such abusive license terms. Therefore, the abusive license terms can be forced on the users by the patent holder's arbitrary conduct.

3-2   Anti-competitive Effect in the Market: Provider Case and Non-provider Case

In addition to the above, the following two scenarios will be expected of the anti-competitive effect caused by a refusal of license for IP rights incorporated in standard technology.

One case is that the patent holder providing a product or service incorporating the standard technology refuses to grant a license, and this refusal of license thereby restraints the competition in the relevant market (hereinafter 'Provider case'). In this situation, the patent holder normally refuses its license with its arbitrary conduct for the purpose of extending its superior position to the product or service market.

We can observe, in the Provider case, that the patent holder's conduct will restrict the competition among providers of the product or service and impair the efficiency of the relevant market. Accordingly, the anti-competitive effect of the patent holder's refusal of license is clear in this Provider case.

On the other hand, the anti-competitive effect is not very clear in the case when the patent holder is not the provider of a product or service incorporating the standard technology (hereinafter 'Non-Provider case'). We should note, in the Non-provider case, that this kind of refusal of license may not directly influence the competition in the product or service market. In other words, the effect of restraint of competition among those providers caused by the refusal of license may not be immediately identified if the patent holder's refusal does not involve any arbitrary conduct.

In this Non-provider case, however, some scholars in Japanese academia suggest that the patent holder's 'opportunism' will make the scale of those providers' investment smaller than the scaled-up investment under a status of the competitive market due to the providers' preparatory cost for the patent holder's possible opportunistic conduct[3]. This may consequently impair the efficiency of the product or service market from a

3.Yanagawa, *Torihikihiyou keizaigaku to yuuetsuteki chii no ranyou*[*Transaction cost economy and abuse of bargaining power*] 697 Kouseitorihiki 8, 9 (2008) [hereinafter *Yanagawa*].

long-term viewpoint.

3-3 Summary

As stated in this section, the anti-competitive aspect can be analyzed in accordance with the combination of the right holder's position in the standard setting process, i.e., the Insider situation, the Outsider situation or the Ambush situation, and the right holder's position in the relevant market, i.e., the Provider or the Non-Provider case. The next section will examine how the Japanese AMA evaluate these anti-competitive effects caused by a refusal of license in each situation.

4 Overview of Japanese AMA

In order toconsider the regulation of the Insider situation, the Outsider situation and the Ambush situation under the Japanese AMA, it is first necessary to examine the objectives of the Japanese AMA. This section will examine the details of its objectives and explain its three types of regulations.

4-1 Primary Objectives in Article 1 of the AMA : 'Fair and Free Competition' and 'Consumer's Interests'

It is the common understanding in academia that the AMA will 'promote fair and free competition' as Article 1 of the AMA sets out. Through achieving this primary objective, the AMA shall ultimately 'improve the level of employment and net national income' and 'ensure consumer's interests and promote a democratic and sound development of domestic economy'. Academia insists that the objective to 'promote fair and free competition' is the primary objective of the AMA, and the rest of the objectives under Article 1 are the secondary objectives to be achieved through protection of the primary objective[4].

4-1-1 Promoting the Fair and Free Competition

The AMA provides that, as stated in the above, the primary purpose of AMA is to 'promote fair and free competition'. This means to protect the consumer's interests through the market competition which adjusts price and quality of products or services in the market. The details of this primary purpose should be interpreted through the

---

4.Imamura, Dokusenkinshi hou nyuumon [Introduction of Anti-Monopoly Act] (1993) 2 [hereinafter *Imamura*], Kanai, Kawahama & Sensui, Dokusenkinshi hou [Antimonopoly Act] (6th ed. 2018) 4-5 [hereinafter *Kanai, Kawahama & Sensui*].*See* Judgement of Supreme Court (Oil Price Cartel), 24 Feb 1984, 38-4 Keishu 1287 .

theory of economics[5].

4-1-2 Avoiding the Inefficiency and Social Cost

If there exists a monopoly status in the market, the dominant enterprise will be able to obtain the power to control the market and maintain its dominant price. The control of the dominant price will lead to a transfer of the surplus from consumer to supplier and create a loss of economic welfare in the market. In other words, the loss and transfer constitute both the inefficiency in resource allocation and the additional social cost in market transactions. It is an objective of the AMA to avoid such inefficiency and social cost caused by the dominant enterprise's market power[6].

4-1-3 Protecting the Consumer's Interests

In addition to the objectives above, it is also the objective of the AMA to protect the consumer's interests and its efficiency in resource allocation.

It is in the consumer's best interests to purchase products at the equilibrium price which should be at a lower price than the dominant price, and obtain a larger volume of products or services at the equilibrium supply output which should be at a larger output level than the dominant supply output level, through the competitive market mechanism. Thus, it is possible to say that an objective of the AMA is to protect the consumer's interests by maintaining the equilibrium price and the equilibrium output level in the market[7]. However, it should be remembered that academia regards this objective as a secondary objective of the AMA which should be achieved by the primary objective, i.e., 'promoting fair and free competition' [8].

4-1-4 Promoting the Technological Innovation and Dynamic Competition

Some academic opinions have recently insisted that dynamic competition should be emphasized as one of the objectives of the AMA. Those opinions believe that, when the competition becomes inactive in the market, the incentive for technological innovation will be also impaired. On the other hand, another academic opinion claims that a dominant enterprise can instead make technological innovation more active in the market[9].

5.Judgement of Tokyo High Court, 19 Sep 1951, 4-14 Koumin 497 (Toho/Subaru case), Judgement of Tokyo High Court, 7 Dec 1953, 4-12 Gyoushu 3215 (Toho/Shintoho case). *See* Shiraishi, Gijyutsu to kyousou no houtekikouzou [Legal structure of technology and competition] (1994) 43-50 [hereinafter *Shiraishi*], Wakui, Gijutsu hyoujun wo meguru hou sisutemu [Law system regarding technological standards] (2010) 47-48 [hereinafter *Wakui*].

6.*Kanai, Kawahama & Sensui* at 8.

7.*Id.* at 9.

8.*See Id.* at 4-5, *Imamura* at 2.

9.*Kanai, Kawahama & Sensui* at 10.

In terms of this discussion, we should also note that the JFTCidentifies the element of 'effect of promoting the competition in the R&D market' in the guideline for its judgement of the restraint of competition in the market and takes account of this factor in their analysis[10].

4-1-5 Summary

As examined in this section, it is the characteristics of the Japanese AMA that its primary objective described in the statute is 'promoting the fair and free competition' rather than 'avoiding the market inefficiency' or 'protecting the consumer's interests'. It should be noted that this characteristics can be influential to the authority's approach to the refusal of license for IP rights situation.

The following section will explain the framework of restriction on refusal of license for IP rights under the Japanese AMA.

4-2 Framework of the AMA

4-2-1 Private Monopolization and Unfair Trade Practices

Under the Japanese AMA, the refusal of license conducted by a sole entity can constitute a violation of Private Monopolization or Unfair Trade Practices.

Firstly, 'Private Monopolization' in Article 3 forepart of the AMA means that 'such business activities, by which any entrepreneur, individually or by combination or conspiracy with other entrepreneurs, or by any other manner, excludes or controls the business activities of other entrepreneurs, thereby causing, contrary to the public interest, a substantial restraint of competition in any particular field of trade' in Article 2-5 of the AMA. This concept of Private Monopolization comes from the US Antitrust Law's restriction of 'Monopolization' in Article 2 of its Sherman Act[11].

The refusal of license for IP rights by a sole IP rights owner can be regarded as a kind of 'refusal of trade' under the AMA. Accordingly, if there exists a refusal of license which a) excludes other entities' business activities from the market, and b) causes substantial restraint of competition in the relevant market, such a refusal of license can constitute a conduct of 'Private Monopolization' and a violation of Article 3 forepart of the AMA[12].

Secondly, 'Unfair Trade Practices' in Article 19 of the AMA means 'any act falling under

---

10.*JFTC IP Guideline* at Section 3-1.

11.*Kanai, Kawahama & Sensui* at 148.

12.On the other hand, if refusal of trade or license is a joint boycott, the regulation under 'Unreasonable Restraint of Trade' (Article 3 rearpart, AMA) can be applied to the refusal.

any of following items, which is designated by the Fair Trade Commission as the possible unfair conducts in Article 2-9 of the AMA: (i) Unjustly treating other entrepreneurs in a discriminatory manner; (ii) Dealing with unjust consideration; (iii) Unjustly inducing or coercing customers of a competitor to deal with oneself; (iv) Dealing with another party on such conditions as it will unjustly restrict the business activities of the said party; (v) Dealing with another party by unjust use of one's bargaining position; or (vi) Unjustly interfering with a transaction between an entrepreneur in competition with it in Japan with oneself or a corporation of which oneself is a stockholder or an officer and another transaction counter party; or, in case such entrepreneur is a corporation, unjustly inducing, instigating, or coercing a stockholder or an director of such corporation to act against the interests of such corporation'.

According to the understanding of the Report of Anti-Monopoly Act Study Group (1982)[13], the 'fair competition' to be protected by the Unfair Trade Practicesregulation under the AMA will be maintained by protection of the following three statuses in the market: a) the free competitionamong entities in the market is not impaired and an entity's entry into the market is not blocked (hereinafter 'Freedom of Competition'), b) the free competition is working on the basis of the price, quality or service (hereinafter 'Competition on Merit'), and c) the foundation of free competition on which entities in the market can decide to enter a deal or accept its contract terms by their own decision is secured (hereinafter 'Foundation of Free Competition'). This report insists that the 'fair competition' in the market will be guaranteed by the protection of all three statuses.

Firstly, the typical conduct impairing the 'Freedom of Competition' status is an attempt to obtain market power. If an entity which does not have a dominant position in the market tries to unjustly obtain market power, such conduct shall be regarded as conduct restraining the status of 'Freedom of Competition'. In this regard, academic opinions point out that there are many similarities between the Unfair Trade Practicesregulation of the Japanese AMA and the Unfair Method of Competition regulation under Article 5 of the FTC Act in the US Antitrust Law[14].

Secondly, the reasonable competition based on the price, quality or service is required for maintaining the status of 'Competition on Merit'. The typical conducts restraining the 'Competition on Merit' are as follows: a) disturbing other entities' reasonable

---

decision-making (e.g., false trades, or compulsory trades), and b) damaging competitor's market activity (e.g., interference with competitor's market activities, or interference with competitor's decision-making).

Lastly, the uniqueness of the status of 'Foundation of Free Competition' should be remarked. The typical conduct impairing the 'Foundation of Free Competition' can be found in the situation where an entity intrudes upon other entities' decision-making about accepting contract terms of trade. This conduct is normally categorized as the conduct of 'abuse of superior bargaining position' in Article 2-9-(v) of the AMA.

It should be noted that the violation of 'Foundation of Free Competition' does not mandatorily require a clear restraint of market competition among other entities caused by superior entity's conduct. This is a characteristic of 'Foundation of Free Competition' which is largely different from the above-mentioned two categories.

In this regard, academic opinions insist that the dominant entity's opportunistic conduct in a continuing relationship (e.g., change of transaction conditions in a long-term business contract) is the typical case of impairment of the 'Foundation of Free Competition'. Also, we should remark as well that such superior entity's opportunistic conduct may make the other entities' transaction cost higher, and this will lead to a decrease in the other entities' investment level and a loss of economic welfare in the market[15].

Overall, we can conclude that the Unfair Trade Practicesregulation under the AMA deals with the attempts made by an entity to obtain or extend the market power and other anti-competitive conducts which are uniquely identified in the Japanese AMA.

4-2-2   Restriction on Refusal of License for IP Rights

Sole refusal of license for IP rights can typically constitute a conduct of 'Other Refusal to Trade'[1]in Article 2 of the Designation of Unfair Trade Practices(hereinafter 'General Designation')[17]covering Article 2-9-(i) ('(i) Unjustly treat other entrepreneurs in a discriminatory manner') of the AMA under the Unfair Trade Practices regulation. Also, the sole refusal of license may be confirmed as a conduct of the Private Monopolization in Article 3 forepart of the AMA, if the refusing party maintains the dominant market position.

If a refusal of license for IP rights is made for the purpose of excluding competitors from

---

15.*Yanagawa* at 9.

16.Article 2 (Other Refusal to Trade), Designation of Unfair Trade Practices '(2) Unjustly refusing to trade, or restricting the quantity or content of goods or services for trade with a certain enterprise, or causing another enterprise to engage in any conduct that falls under one of these practices'.

17.Designation of Unfair Trade Practices, Fair Trade Commission Public Notice No. 15 of 1982.

the market or other unjust purposes, an impediment of the 'fair competition' under the Unfair Trade Practicesregulation, and a violation of the AMA, caused by the refusal of license will be confirmed.

Also, if a dominant entity uses a refusal of license for its IP rights for the purpose of extending or maintaining its dominant position in the market, such a refusal of license will constitute a conduct of the Private Monopolization and a violation of the AMA.

As explained in the above, refusal of license can constitute a violation of the Private Monopolization regulation or the Unfair Trade Practices regulation under the AMA, if there exists the market power or the probability of obtaining the market power with the refusing entity. In addition, we should note on the uniqueness of the Japanese AMA that, even if there exits no clear restraint of market competition among other entities, sole refusal of license can constitute a violation of the Unfair Trade Practices regulation as a conduct impeding the 'Foundation of Free Competition'.

On the other hand, it should be also remarked that the Japanese AMA has another important provision of the exemption of 'the conducts recognizable as exercise of rights' in Article 21 of the AMA in terms with its restriction on the refusal of license for IP rights. The next section will explain this exemption from the scope of the AMA.

4-2-3   Article 21 of the AMA: Exemption of 'the conducts recognizable as exercise of rights'

As stated in the previous section, there exists a possibility that refusal of license for IP rights can constitute a violation of Article 3 forepart or Article 19 of the AMA. However, on the other hand, Article 21 of the AMA provides the basic principle that the lawful exercise of IP rights shall be exempted from the regulations under the AMA.

Article 21 of the AMA provides that 'the provisions of this Act shall not apply to such conducts recognizable as the exercise of rights under CopyrightsAct, Patents Act, Utility Model Rights Act, Design Rights Act, or TrademarkAct'.

This article means that the AMA shall not be applied to 'the conducts recognizable as exercise of rights' which are protected under the IP law in Japan. The judgement of whether a conduct should be regarded as 'the conducts recognizable as exercise of rights' or not will be normally made on the basis of the appearance of conduct. However, if the result of a conduct is against the purposes of the IP law system, such a conduct will not be regarded as 'the conducts recognizable as exercise of rights'[18].

18.Atsuya, Dokusenkinshi hou nyuumon [Introduction of Antimonopoly Act] (7th ed, 2012) 122 (hereinafter *Atsuya*). *Kanai, Kawahama & Sensui* at 398-399.

While a clear definition of the 'exercise of rights' itself is not provided in the AMA, academia regards 'the conducts recognizable exercise of rights' as the rights holder's lawful enforcement of rights which intends to exclude other parties' unauthorized use of IP rights. The typical examples of those conducts are as follows: a) claiming an injunction against an IP infringer, b) refusal to grant a license to an IP infringer, or c) limiting the terms of IP license granted to a licensee.

However, it should be noted that IP holder's conduct may not constitute 'the conducts recognizable as exercise of rights', when a result of the conduct is against the purposes of the IP law system, even if an appearance of the conduct fits one of the above three categories. In this regard, each purpose of the IP law system should be identified individually on the basis of the nature of each IP right, such as patents right, copyrights, design right or other IP rights[19].

More specifically, the primary purpose of the Patents Law of Japan is described as follows: 'through promoting protection and utilization of inventions, to encourage the creation of inventions and thereby to contribute to the development of industry' (Article 1, Patents Act of Japan). The growth of the economy through the protection of the creation of technological ideas is the purpose of the Patents Law[20]. On the other hand, the primary purpose of the CopyrightsLaw of Japan is explained as follows: '⋯ giving due regard to the fair exploitation of these cultural products, and by doing so, to contribute to the development of culture' (Article 1, CopyrightsAct of Japan). The promotion of cultural activities through the protection of creative works is the purpose of the Copyrights Law[21].

As explained in the above, Article 21 of the Japanese AMA indicates that the lawful exercise of IP rights should be exempted from a scope of the AMA, as far as the exercise is not against the purposes of the IP law system. Then, more specifically, what is the borderline between those conducts in accordance with the purposes of the IP law system and the other conducts against such purposes? The next section will examine this question through an analysis of the cases and guidelines in Japan.

19.*Wakui* at 176, also see *JFTC IP Guideline* at Section 2-1.

20.Tamura, Chiteki zaisann hou [Intellectual Property Law] (2d ed, 2000) 152 (hereinafter *Tamura*).

21.*Id.* at 358-359.

5　Cases in Japan

5-1　Overall

In the Japanese AMA there exist a number of cases of the sole refusals of trade for tangible assets and one case of the joint refusal of license for IP rights[22]as well as several cases of the tie-in or cartel arrangements involving refusal of license. This chapter will extract the common criteria from the decisions of those cases[23].

5-2　Abstract of Cases

5-2-1　Cases of Refusal of Trade for Tangible Assets

Prior to an analysis of the refusal of license for IP rights cases, this section will examine the refusal of trade for tangible assets cases for the purpose of clarifying the basic principle of the AMA's regulation on the sole refusal situation.

In the Yukijirushi Milk case (1956)[24], the JFTCindicated that Yukijirushi Milk and Hokkaido Butter made Norinchukin Bank refuse to provide a financial loan with a farmer's association providing the raw milk to their competitors in the market and maintained their dominant market position through this conduct. The JFTC concluded that their conduct constituted a violation of the Private Monopolization regulation in Article 3 forepart of the AMA and a violation of the Unfair Trade Practicesas a conduct of 'Refusal of Trade' in Article 1 of its former General Designation (1953). This is the basic case of refusal of trade which involves clear restraint of the market competition among the related parties and their competitors in the market.

Following the above, it should be noted that in the Marukame Fruiterer case (1972)[25]and the Noevia Cosmetics case (2002)[26]the JFTCand the High Court indicated that the asset owner's refusal of trade can constitute a violation of the Unfair Trade Practicesregulation, even though a clear negative effect to competition among the

---

22.Apple vs. Samsung case (2014) involving SEP in the IP High Court of Japan was a case of the abuse of rights under Article 1-3 of Civil Code, as apposed to a case of the violation of AMA. Also, One-Blue LLC Case (2016) [Announcement of JFTC, Breach of Anti-monopoly Act by One-Blue LLC, 18 Nov. 2016] involving SEP is a decision of Article 14 'Interference with a Competitor's Transactions' of the General Designation in the Unfair Trade Practices regulation to be introduced in the later chapter.

23.Mukai, Kyousouhou ni okeru kyousei raisensutou no jitsumu [Compulsory license under Anti-monopoly Act] (2010) 175 [hereinafter *Mukai*].

24.Decision (trial) of JFTC, 28 Jul 1956, 8 Shinketsushu 12 (hereinafter *Yukijirushi Case*).

25.Decision (trial) of JFTC, 19 Apr 1967, 14 Shinketsushu 64 (Marukame Fruiterer case) [hereinafter *Marukame Fruiterer Case*].

26.Judgement of Tokyo High Court, 5 Dec 2002, 1814 Hanreijihou 82 (Noevia Cosmetics case) [hereinafter *Noevia Cosmetics Case*].

entities competing in the upstream market or the downstream market could not be confirmed.

In the Marukame Fruiterer case, a wholesaler in the Marukame fruits market refused to provide its products to a distributor which was against the wholesaler's decisions within the fruit shops association. JFTCconfirmed wholesaler's refusal of trade as a violation of the Unfair Trade Practices regulation, even though the wholesaler's refusal to provide its products was made solely for the purpose of controlling the decision making in internal conferences of the fruits shops association in the market, and a clear negative effect to competition among the entities competing in the relevant markets could not be found[27]. Also, in the Noevia Cosmetics case a cosmetics products manufacturer refused to provide its products to an distributor company for the purpose of retaliating against the distributor's claim on its no-return policy under the existing transaction contract terms. The Tokyo High Court concluded the manufacturer was in violation of the Unfair Trade Practices regulation as a conduct of 'Other Refusal to Trade' in Article 2 of its General Designation covering Article 2-9-(i) of the AMA.

This means that JFTCand the High Court do not mandatorily require a clear negative effect to competition among the entities competing in the upstream market or the downstream market (hereinafter 'Negative Competitive Effect among the Competitors') for confirming a refusal of trade as a violation of the Unfair Trade Practicesregulation under the AMA. In other words, they may conclude its violation under a situation where a) a refusal of trade is made by a refusing party with the malicious intent of damaging the refused party's business continuance and b) where any damage to a refused party's business continuance is caused by the refusal.

5-2-2   Discussion of the Japanese Essential Facilities Doctrine

In the NTT Eastern Japan case (2010)[28]the JFTCfound a violation of the Private Monopolization regulation in a refusal of granting an access to the facility under the fair terms by NTT Eastern Japan, which owned a fiber optic network facility in the upstream market and provided its own communication service in the downstream market, and placed upon the NTT Eastern Japan an obligation to grant access to its facility to other entities in the downstream market, and the Supreme Court confirmed the JFTC's ruling. A scholarly opinion insists that this decision can be categorized in a case of the Japanese Essential Facilitiesapproach[29]to be applied in the following situation: a) a party holding

---

27.In this case the refusing party was not an entity competing in the downstream market. Also, the refusal of trade did not maintain or strengthen refusing party's market position in the upstream market.

28.Judgement of Supreme Court, 17 Dec 2010, 57 Shinektsushu 215 (NTT Eastern Japan case).

29.Tanaka, *Kiseikanawsijyou heno sannyu to dokusentekichii no ranyou*[*Entry into liberalized markets and abuse of dominant position*] 38-1 Kobegakuin Hougaku 151, 155-156 (2008), *available at* http://www.law-kobegakuin.jp/~jura/law/files/38-1-04.pdf.

its dominant position in the upstream market owns the facility which constitutes the essential element for entering into the downstream market, and b) the said party refuses to grant access to the facility to other entities or permits access to them under inferior terms to its own terms[30].

However, we should note that this case still maintained the traditional definition of 'relevant market' and did not employ the exceptionally narrow definition of 'relevant market' which has been developed in the European Essential Facilitiesdoctrine under the EU Competition Law[31]. Also the refusing party in this case provided its own service in the downstream market, and its refusal was made for the purpose of extending the refusing party's market position to the downstream market.

In summary, it is the author's opinion that this NTT Eastern Japan case should be categorized in one of the traditional Private Monopolization cases in which a dominant party attempts to extend its market position to the downstream market through the refusal of trade. The decision, in this case, does not involve the characteristics of the European Essential Facilitiesdoctrine to be introduced in a later chapter.

As examined above, in the Japanese refusal of trade for tangible assets cases the requirement of the 'Negative Competitive Effect among the Competitors' is not mandatory under the Unfair Trade Practicesregulation, as we can see this characteristic in the Marukame Fruiterer case and the Noevia Cosmetics case. Also, we should note that the Japanese AMA does not employ an approach of the European Essential Facilitiesdoctrine in the refusal of trade cases.

5-2-3 Cases of Joint Refusal of License for IP Rights

Following an analysis of the refusal of trade cases, this section will analyze the criteria of refusal of license for IP rights cases. There exists a case of joint refusal of license and multiple cases of cartel or tie-in involving IP rights in the Japanese AMA[32].

In the Pachinko Manufacturers' Patent Pool case (1997)[33]the JFTCconcluded that a joint refusal of license by the patents holders to future entrants into a product market of Pachinko pinball machines constitutes a violation of the Private Monopolization regulation (Article 3 forepart, AMA). It should be remarked in this case that, because of

---

30.*Id.*

31.*Shiraishi* at 72-74, *Kanai, Kawahama & Sensui* at 291-292.

32.Judgement of Tokyo High Court, 1 Nov 2013, 2206 Hanreijihou 37 (E-License case)(2013) where a bundle license policy of music copyrights constituted Private Monopolization should be categorized in a conduct of Exclusive Dealing, as opposed to Refusal of License. This chapter will not therefore introduce this case.

33.Decision (recommendation) of JFTC, 6 Aug 1997, 44 Shinketsushu 238 (Pachinko Manufacturers' Patent Pool case) [hereinafter *Pachinko Manufacturers' Patent Pool Case*].

substantial restraint of competition in a technology marketcaused by the patent pool arrangement, new entry into the product market of Pachinko Pinball machines was technically impossible without the license of those patents, and the competition in the downstream market was largely restricted.

Consequently, the JFTCconcluded that patents holders' refusal of license constituted a violation of the AMA.

5-2-4 Cases of Cartel or Tie-in Involving IP Rights

In the Concrete Pile case (1970)[34]the JFTCdecided to abolish a commitment to the restrictive license policy of cartel members' patents in the cartel case as a violation of the Unreasonable Restraint of Trade regulation (Article 3 rearpart, AMA).

The JFTCconfirmed that substantial restraint of competition in the relevant market was caused by the cartel arrangement involving a commitment of restrictive license policy to other entities for cartel member's holding patents, and it was technically difficult for other entities to enter the market without the patent license due to their patents concentration in this case[35].

Following the above, in the Fukuoka City Public Sewer case (1993)[36], a cartel case involving refusal of license for the existing competitors, use of a utility model right held by Hinode Water Supply Products company was an essential element for a new entrant into the market. It was technically impossible for other entities to provide their products in the product market, since Fukuoka city maintained its requirement specification in the bidding process which obliged the use of the Hinode utility model right.

The JFTC confirmed the substantial restraint of competition in the relevant market caused by the cartel arrangement involving a restrictive license policy for the utility model right. It thus concluded that the cartel arrangement constituted a violation of the Unreasonable Restraint of Trade regulation (Article 3 rearpart, AMA), and the arrangement involving the restrictive license policy should be abandoned[37].

Finally, in the MicrosoftJapan case (1998)[38], a tie-in case involving the refusal of

---

34.Decision (recommendation) of JFTC, 5 Aug 1970, 17 Shinketsushu 86 (Concrete Pile case) [hereinafter *Concrete Pile Case*].

35.*See Mukai* at 233.

36.Decision (recommendation) of JFTC, 10 Sep 1993, 40 Shinketsushu 3 (Fukuoka City Public Water case) [hereinafter *Fukuoka City Public Water Case*].

37.Aoyagi, *Saikousuuryouseigen to OEM seizouitakugimu no dokukinnhoujyou no hyouka*[*Analysis under AMA on limitation of maximum volume and OEM manufacturing contract obligation*], 20 Chitekizaisannhou seisakugaku kenkyu 299, 323-324 (2008), *available at* https://eprints.lib.hokudai.ac.jp/dspace/bitstream/2115/43570/1/20_299-353.pdf.

38.Decision (recommendation) of JFTC, 14 Dec 1998, 45 Shinketsushu 153 (Microsoft Japan case) [hereinafter *Microsoft Japan Case*].

license, the JFTCconfirmed that Microsoft Japan's (hereinafter 'MSJ') spreadsheet application software maintained a large market share in the spreadsheet application software market, and it was difficult for PC manufacturers to pre-install the spreadsheet application software in their PCs without the software license from MSJ. Also, we should note that there could be the network effects existing among the users of MSJ's spreadsheet application software.

Under the circumstances, the JFTC concluded that MSJ's tie-in strategy, between its spreadsheet application software and other software, involving the refusal of license for its spreadsheet application software should be regarded as a conduct of 'Tie-in Sales' in Article 10 of the old General Designation (1982)[39]and constituted a violation of the Unfair Trade Practicesregulation (Article 19, AMA)[40].

5-2-5 Summary of Cases

As examined in this chapter, the joint refusal of license for patents under the situation where the refusing parties competed in the product market was confirmed as a violation of the AMA in the Pachinko Manufacturers' Patent Pool case. In this case negative effect on competition in the downstream market was clear. Also, in the Concrete Pile case and in the Fukuoka City Public Sewer case the restricted license policy for IP rights was for the purpose of maintaining the IP rights holder's market position in the product market, and its negative effect to competition in the downstream market was evident. Similarly, in the MicrosoftJapan case, the restricted license policy for its software was made for a purpose of extending its market position into the market of another product, and its negative effect to competition in the relevant market was also clear.

In summary, the criteria for a violation of the AMA on the sole refusal of license for IP rights case is still unclear from those joint refusal of license cases and cartel or tie-in cases involving IP rights cases in the above. Especially, it is also unclear whether a sole refusal of license for IP rights can constitute a violation of the Unfair Trade Practicesregulation in the AMA under the situation where the refusing party does not compete in the downstream market, and the 'Negative Competitive Effect among the Competitors' in the relevant markets cannot be clearly confirmed.

In terms with this matter, we should recall the refusal of trade cases such as the Marukame Fruiterer case or the Noevia Cosmetics case in which the decision concluded a violation of the Unfair Trade Practicesregulation without confirming the 'Negative

---

39.Designation of Unfair Trade Practices, Fair Trade Commission Public Notice No. 15 of 1982.

40.Ishioka, *Hyoukeisan sofuto to tano sofuto no dakiawase hanbai*[*Tie-in sales between spreadsheet software and other software*], *in* Keizaihou hanrei shinketsu hyakusen [Selected judges and decisions in economics law] 128, 128,*Kanai, Kawahama & Sensui* at 377.

Competitive Effect among the Competitors' in the relevant markets.

The next chapter will introduce scholarly opinions regarding this question and try to clarify the criteria for a violation of the AMA on the sole refusal of license for IP rights case.

5-3   Analysis and Scholarly Opinions

5-3-1   'Negative Competitive Effect among the Competitors' in Refusal of Trade Case and 'Refusal of Trade as Abuse of Superior Position'

In the refusal of trade for tangible assets cases, such as the Marukame Fruits case and the Noevia Cosmetics case, the JFTCand the high court confirmed that the refusal of trade constitutes a violation of the Unfair Trade Practices regulation under the situation where the refuser, maintaining a superior position in the upstream market, does not conduct business in the downstream market. For example, Marukame's refusal to provide its fruits products was solely for controlling the decision-making in the market association's internal conference. This refusal did not involve a clear negative effect on competition among the entities in the relevant market[41].

It is the author's understanding in those cases that the JFTCcategorized this refusal of trade, involving no clear 'Negative Competitive Effect among the Competitors' in the relevant markets, in a conduct of the Refusal of Trade as Abuse of Superior Position[42]and intervenes in this exceptional refusal of trade situation in order to protect the 'Foundation of Free Competition' [43]which is explained as one of the purposes of AMA in the previous chapter[44].

Under this Refusal of Trade as Abuse of Superior Positionregulation an owner of an asset maintaining the superior position in the market will be obliged to provide the asset to other entities under the non-discriminatory terms, and only in the exceptional situation where the reasonable discriminatory terms based on each procurement cost can be identified will those discriminatory terms of trade be permissible under the AMA[45]. Also, we should note that JFTC's Study Group Report (1987) insists that the Refusal of Trade as Abuse of Superior Positionregulation should be applied to situations where a refusal

---

41.Negishi & Funada, Dokusenkinshi hou gaisetsu [Abstract of Antimonopoly Act] 198-199 (5th ed. 2015) [hereinafter *Negishi & Funada*], Sanekata, Dokusenkinshi hou [Anti-monopoly Act] 206-207 (4th ed.1998) [hereinafter*Sanekata*]. Also *See AMA Report 1982* at 6-7.

42.*See Kanai, Kawahama & Sensui* at 290-291.

43.*See Kanai, Kawahama & Sensui* at 31-32.

44.On the other hand, a refusal of license involving 'Negative Competitive Effect among the Competitors' in the relevant markets should be categorized in the Refusal of Trade as Impedance of Freedom of Competition which protects the 'Freedom of Competition' as another purpose of AMA.

45.*Negishi & Funada* at 203-204, *Sanekata* at 207.

is related to the fair competition order, and this judgement of 'relation with the fair competition order' should be made in light of the scale of disadvantage or influence caused by a refusal of trade[46].

5-3-2　Refusal of License Case under Article 21 of AMA and 'Refusal of Trade as Abuse of Superior Position'

If we can simply rely on the authority's approach in the cases of refusal of trade for tangible asset as Refusal of Trade as Abuse of Superior Position, it should be presumed that the AMA will be able to intervene in a refusal of license for IP rights under the situation where the 'Negative Competitive Effect among the Competitors' in the relevant markets cannot be found.

However, can this presumption be acceptable in light of a proper interpretation of Article 21 ('exemption for the conducts recognizable as exercise of IP rights') of the AMA? We should note on the cases of refusal of trade for tangible assets that the authority's intervention in an asset owner's freedom of trade does not largely change an asset owner's market position.　In the market of tangible assets, an owner of an asset constantly faces the market competition, and the asset owner's position of dominance is not guaranteed.

On the other hand, in the cases of refusal of license for IP rights, such as patents or copyrights, an IP rights holder invests its economic and moral cost in creating technologies or creations protected by the IP rights and expects to obtain exclusive income derived from the use of technologies or creations for the purpose of recovering the economic and moral cost[47].　The IP law system has firmly guaranteed this core concept to inventors or creators of IP rights since its establishment in the late 19[th]century[48]. Accordingly, the AMA's intervention in the refusal of license cases could largely impair IP rights holder's expected income and incentive for future investment of its economic and moral cost in creating new technologies or creations[49].

In terms with this matter, it is author's opinion that the AMA should intervene in refusal of license for IP rights only in the situation where there exists the clear Negative Competitive Effect among the Competitors in the relevant markets, since the core concept of the IP law system should be largely respected under the provision of Article 21

46.*AMA Report 1982* at 5.

47.*Wakui* at 241-242.

48.*Cf.* Exclusive Patents Regulations (1885), Publishing Regulations (1863).

49.*Wakui* at 243.

of the AMA[50], which the AMA has firmly maintained as its premise with the IP law system since the mid 20[th]century[51], and a balance between protection of market competition and incentive to technological development[52]should be carefully maintained. Accordingly, the author believes that the AMA should not intervene in a refusal of license case for the reason of the Refusal of Trade as Abuse of Superior Positionunder the Unfair Trade Practicesregulation, and an owner of IP rights maintaining the superior position in the market should not be obliged to grant a license to other entities under the non-discriminatory terms.

In this regard, Takigawa indicates his concern about the regulation of Unfair Trade Practicesto the refusal of trade cases[53]. He points out the risk of a broad application of the Unfair Trade Practicesregulation in refusal of trade case and states that 'since sole refusal of trade is a substantial element of entity's freedom of market activities, the AMA should not interfere with the sole refusal of trade unless there exists a refusal of trade made by an entity maintaining the dominant market power. This means the JFTCshould abolish the Unfair Trade Practice regulation on sole refusal of trade cases and solely maintain the Private Monopolization regulation on those cases'.
Takigawa expresses his clear concern about the regulation on refusal of trade cases in view of the balance between protection of market competition and an entity's right of freedom of trade[54]. Takigawa's concern should be more emphasized in refusal of license cases.

Also, Kawahama expresses his concern regarding the negative effect to asset owner's incentives to future investment caused by asset owner's obligation of providing non-discriminatory access to other entities under the Essential Facilitiesdoctrine in refusal of trade cases[55]. Kawahama's concern should be more emphasized in refusal of license cases as well.

Furthermore, Wakui indicates that 'the IP law system is designed on the basis of the theory that it is more beneficial for economic welfare in the society to permit an opportunity of obtaining excessive profit beyond competition level to inventors of new technologies. Accordingly, Wakui further insists that 'the AMA's intervention in IP

50.*Cf.* Article 23 of the old AMA (before the revision of 2000).

51.*Cf.* Anti-monopoly Act of Japan (1947).

52.*See Greenhalgh & Rogers* at 27, for micro economics analysis.

53.Takigawa, Nichibei EU no dokukinhou to kyousou seisaku [Competition law in Japan, US and EU and competition policy] (3d ed. 2006) 275 (hereinafter *Takigawa 2006*).

54.*Takigawa 2006* at 274.

55.*Kanai, Kawahama & Sensui* at 291-292.

rights holder's lawful conduct pursuing excessive profit is not appropriate, since it is lawfully expected for an IP rights holder under the IP law system to obtain excessive profit beyond competitive level'[56]. In other words, IP rights holder's lawful opportunistic conduct for pursuing extra revenue is encouraged under the IP law system, and IP rights holders should have a lawful right to recover the economic and moral cost invested in its technological development work or creative work.

5-3-3 Summary

In summary, it is the author's opinion that the AMA should not intervene in sole refusal of license for IP rights cases by a reason of the Refusal of Trade as Abuse of Superior Positionin the Unfair Trade Practicesregulation under the situation of no 'Negative Competitive Effect among the Competitors' in the relevant markets, unless there exists any clear 'anti-competitive arbitrary conduct' in the market. IP rights owners should not be obliged to grant a non-discriminatory license of their rights to other entities.

Then what is the 'anti-competitive arbitrary conduct' in the market under a refusal of license situation? The next chapter will confirm JFTCguidelines and try to find possible answers from the guidelines.

6 Guidelines in Japan

6-1 Overall

Based on the decisions in the previous cases, the Japanese FTC (hereinafter 'JFTC') announces their guidelines on the IP rights enforcement. This section will focus on the details of those guidelines regarding refusal of license for the IP rights related to standard technology and find an answer to the question of 'anti-competitive arbitrary conduct' .

The JFTC guidelines are JFTC's declarations on its AMA regulation policy to all entities in the market. Also, those guidelines are announced for the purpose of clarifying a safe harbour of entity conduct. It is the basic principle that the JFTC will not prosecute an entity's conducts if they follow the guidelines[57]. However, although the Japanese court pays due attention to statements in JFTCguidelines, those guidelines have no legally binding effects on future judgement by the court[58].

56.*Wakui* at 241-242.

57.*Shirasihi* at 380 & 389-390.

58.*Shirasihi* at 380.

6-2   Details of JFTC Guidelines

6-2-1   JFTC Guidelines for Patent and Know-how Licensing Agreements (1999)

The JFTCpublished their 'Guidelines for Patent and Know-How Licensing Agreements' in 1999, and indicated their opinion on the refusal of license in 'Understanding of Private Monopolization and patent and know-how licensing agreements (Section 3-3)'. In this guideline, the JFTC stated that 'when a rights holder uses its patent rights as its unreasonable rhetoric for refusal of license, and their refusal of license is against a purpose of technologies protection system. Such refusal of license should not be regarded as the 'conducts recognizable as exercise of right'[59].

6-2-2   AMA Reform Proposal in JFTC Anti-Monopoly Act Study Group Report (2003)

The JFTC's 'Anti-Monopoly Act Study Group Report' (hereinafter 'JFTC Study Report') in 2003 presented a possible definition of the Japanese Essential Facilitiesdoctrine and proposed new legislation reform for this doctrine.

The report stated that the Essential Facilities in the market should be confirmed under the situation where a) the facilities, rights or information works involve a natural monopoly or the network effects, and the facilities, rights or information works, involve the rare resources exclusively designated by the government or other public sectors, b) use of the facilities is essential for providing services or products in the market, and c) it is extremely difficult for other entities in the market to establish the same facilities due to economical, technical or legal reasons[60].

It should be remarked that this report insists that, even if there is a negative influence for the long-term incentive for those facilities holders, when the scale of the relevant market is very large, and the competitive benefit caused by granting access to the facilities is substantial, a grant of access to the facilities should be obliged to an owncr of the facilities.

However, this proposal of new legislation reform in the AMA was finally abandoned by the JFTCafter careful discussion.

6-2-3   JFTC Guidelines for the Use of Intellectual Property under the Anti-Monopoly Act (2007, Revised 2010, 2016)

The new guideline 'Guidelines for the Use of Intellectual Property under the Anti-Monopoly Act' (hereinafter 'IP Guidelines') presented by the JFTCin 2007 clarified

---

59.Japan Fair Trade Commission, *Guidelines for Patent and Know-how Licensing Agreements*, 20 Jul 1999, Section 3-3 [hereinafter *JFTC Patent Know-how Guideline*].

60.JFTC Anti-monopoly Act Study Group, *Dokusenkinshi hou kenkyukai houkokusho* [*Report of Anti-monopoly Act Study Group*], 1 Oct 2003, 51-52 [hereinafter *JFTCAMA Report 2003*].

its principle that refusal of license is a conduct permitted by the IP law system[61]. Thus, in this guideline, a sole refusal of license is primarily categorized in the 'conducts recognizable as exercise of rights' under Article 21 of the AMA[62].

However, some types of a sole refusal of license cannot be regarded as the 'conducts recognizable as exercise of rights', if such conducts are against the purpose of the IP law system, and will constitute a violation of the Private Monopolization regulation or the Unfair Trade Practice regulation under the AMA[63].

Firstly, Section 3-1-i of Part 3 'Viewpoints from Private Monopolization and Unreasonable Restraint of Trade' in the guideline identifies that '(b) Where a technology is found to be influential in a particular product market and is actually used by numerous entrepreneurs in their business activities, it may fall under the exclusion of business activities of other entrepreneurs if any one of the entrepreneurs obtains the rights to the technology from the right-holder and refuses to license the technology to others, preventing them from using it. (Interception)'[64]. The guideline states that the conduct, in this case, can constitute a violation of the Private Monopolization regulation under the AMA. We can observe that the IP Guideline identifies this conduct as a conduct of 'Interception' and a kind of 'anti-competitive arbitrary conduct'[65].

Secondly, the IP Guideline also indicates the case that '(c) In a case in which an entrepreneur conducting business activities in a particular technology or product market collects all of the rights to a technology that may be used by its actual or potential competitors but not for its own use and refuses to license them to prevent the competitors from using the technology, this activity may fall under the exclusion of business activities of other entrepreneurs. (Concentration of rights)'[66]. The guideline states that this conduct can be categorized as a conduct of 'Concentration' and another kind of 'anti-competitive arbitrary conduct'.

Thirdly, the guideline provides '(d) …This also applies in a case in which an entrepreneur holding rights to a technology refuses to grant licenses so as to prevent other entrepreneurs from participating in the bidding after deceiving a public institution into setting out specifications of the product it will be purchasing through bidding that can be satisfied solely by the use of the technology, thereby creating a situation

---

61. *See* Samejima & Yagishita, *Tokkyo raisensu keiyaku no sakusei koushou gyoumu niokeru dokusenkinshi houjyou no mondaiten [Issues on patents license draft and negotiations under AMA]* 64-13 Patent 36 (2011), *available at* https://system.jpaa.or.jp/patents_files_old/201110/jpaapatent201110_036-058.pdf.

62. *JFTC IP Guideline* at Section 3-1.

63. *Id.* at Section 4-5-1.

64. *Id.* at Section 3-1-1-b.

65. *Id.*

66. *Id.* at 3-1-1-c.

in which no bidder can manufacture any product meeting the specifications without receiving the license to use the technology'[67]. This conduct should be categorized as a conduct of 'Deceptive Public Standard Setting' and a kind of 'anti-competitive arbitrary conduct'[68].

In terms of the Unfair Trade Practicesregulation, in Section 4-2 of 'Part 4 Viewpoints from Unfair Trade Practices' the IP Guideline describes the case that '(i) In a case where an entrepreneur acquires the rights to a technology from the right-holder, with the recognition that a competitor uses the licensed technology in its business activities and that it is difficult for the competitor to replace the technology with an alternative, and the entrepreneur refuses to grant a license for it in order to block the competitor from using the technology, this conduct impedes the use of the technology with the intent of interfering with the competitor's business activities'. The guideline states that the conduct, in this case, can constitute a violation of the Unfair Trade Practice regulation under the AMA[69]. This conduct should be regarded as a conduct of 'Acquisition' and a kind of 'anti-competitive arbitrary conduct'.

Furthermore, the guideline also provides that '(ii) When the right-holder to a technology refuses to grant a license to stop other entrepreneurs from using its technology after urging them to use its technology in their business activities through unjustifiable means, such as falsification of licensing conditions, and making it difficult for them to shift to other technology, the conduct unjustifiably creates the status of an infringement on rights and is found to deviate from or run counter to the intents and objectives of the intellectual property systems'[70]. This conduct can constitute a violation of the Unfair Trade Practice regulation and should be regarded as a conduct of 'Lock-in' and another kind of 'anti-competitive arbitrary conduct'.

On the other hand, we should remark that the IP Guideline states that '(iii) In a case where the technology provides the basis for business activities in a particular product market and a number of entrepreneurs, accepting licenses for the technology from

---

67.*Id.* at 3-1-1-d.

68.Section 3-1-1-d of JFTC IP Guideline also provides on 'Deceptive De-jure Standard Setting' that '(d)Under the circumstances in which a product standard has been jointly established by several entrepreneurs, it may fall under the exclusion of the business activities of other entrepreneurs when the right-holder refuses to grant licenses so as to block any development or manufacture of any product compliant with a standard, after pushing for establishment of that standard, which employs a technology of the right-holder, through deceptive means, such as falsification of the licensing conditions applicable in the event the technology is incorporated into the standard, thereby obliging other entrepreneurs to receive a license to use the technology'. This category of arbitrary conduct de-jure standard setting will be explained in the later chapter of Restriction of SEP Enforcement.

69.*JFTC IP Guideline* at Section 4-2-1.

70.*Id.* at Section 4-2-2.

the right-holder, engage in business activities in the product market, the conduct of discriminately refusing to license a particular entrepreneur without reasonable grounds is found to deviate from or run counter to the intent and objectives of the intellectual property systems'[71]. This provision thus insists that IP rights holder's discriminate refusal of license to other entities, a conduct of 'Discriminatory License of Standard Technology', can constitute a violation of the Unfair Trade Practicesregulation solely because the license terms are discriminatory, even though the refusal does not involve any 'anti-competitive arbitrary conducts', such as 'Interception', 'Concentration', 'Deceptive Public Standard Setting', 'Acquisition' or 'Lock-in' as in the above. The situation where a de-facto standard technology is becoming widely accepted through the market competition, and 'the technology provides the basis for business activities in a particular product market and a number of entrepreneurs, ..., engage in business activities in the product market', should not be regarded as a result of 'anti-competitive arbitrary conducts' by IP rights holder.

In terms with this Section 4-2-iii provision of the 'Discriminatory License of Standard Technology' regulation, it is the author's opinion that the AMA should not intervene in sole refusal of license cases by a reason of the Refusal of Trade as Abuse of Superior Positionin the Unfair Trade Practicesregulation unless there exists any clear 'anti-competitive arbitrary conduct' in the market. The author observes some residuals of abandoned discussions on the Japanese Essential Facilitiesdoctrine presented by 'AMA Reform Proposal in JFTCAnti-Monopoly Act Study Group Report (2003)' in this Section 4-2-iii of the IP Guideline. IP rights owners should not be obliged to grant a non-discriminatory license of their rights to other entities under the situation of no 'Negative Competitive Effect among the Competitors' in the relevant markets.

6-2-4　Summary

As examined in the above, the JFTC's IP Guideline admits a possibility that the refusal of license can constitute a violation of AMA by a reason of the Refusal of Trade as Abuse of Superior Positionin the Unfair Trade Practicesregulation, even though there exists no IP rights holder's 'anti-competitive arbitrary conduct' in the market[72].

The author believes that the JFTCshould promptly modify this Section 4-2-iii provision of 'Discriminatory License of Standard Technology' in the guideline and clearly describe a requirement of a clear presence of 'Negative Competitive Effect among the Competitors' in the market for constituting a violation of the Unfair Trade

---

71.*Id.* at Section 4-2-3.

72.*See Id.*

Practicesregulation. This modification of the IP Guideline is necessary for avoiding negative effects on future incentives to technological development in the market.

Regarding this issue, we should remark Wakui's opinion. Wakui indicates that it is not appropriate that an IP rights holder will be obliged to grant a non-discriminatory license under the AMA, even if the IP rights holder obtains its strong market position as a result that a number of entities in the market, and this concern should be emphasized under the situation where those entities using a standard technology should have searched for the existence of the related IP rights.

Wakui further points out as follows[73]. Though Section 3-1 and Section 4-2 of JFTCIP Guideline insists that, when some IP rights become a disseminated fundamental technology for the products in the market, an IP rights holder's discriminatory license policy with no rational reasons can be against the objective of the IP law system, an IP rights holder should not be obliged to grant a non-discriminatory license for its IP rights to the public under the situation where the dissemination of technology does not involve any unlawful arbitrary conduct, and AMA's intervention forcing IP rights holders to grant non-discriminatory licenses can lead to serious impedance to the objectives of the IP law system.

73.*Wakui* at 252-253.

Chapter 3

Restriction of IP Enforcement : Situation in Europe

Following the analysis of the Japanese AMA in the previous chapter, this chapter will consider the current legal approach under the EU Competition Lawand try to determine any implications to the Japanese AMA. The EU Competition Lawhas shown a unique development in its regulation on refusal of license for IP rights.

1   Introduction

As explained in the previous chapter, the refusal of license for IP rights incorporated in standard technology can cause a serious restraint of competition in the market. In this respect, EU Competition lawhas uniquely developed the European Essential Facilitiesdoctrine in the cases of a refusal of trade for international seaport facilities and the Exceptional Circumstances test in the cases of a refusal of license for IP rights.

The European Court of Justice(hereinafter 'ECJ') had developed the 'Exceptional Circumstances' test for the refusal of license cases. Also in the Microsoftcase (2007)[1]and the European Commission's guidance, the more elastic test has been employed for those cases. The author tries to consider the implications to interpretation of the Japanese AMA from the EU Competition Law's approaches to the refusal of license for the IP rights incorporated in standard technology under no Negative Competitive Effect among the Competitors situation.

Accordingly, this chapter will firstly explain the objectives of the EU Competition Law, then examine the EU Competition Law's intervention in the cases of refusal of trade for tangible assets, including the European Essential Facilitiesdoctrine, thirdly analyze the criteria for intervention in the cases of refusal of license for IP rights, such as Magill, IMS, Microsoft, and the European Commission's guidance, and lastly extract implications to interpretation of the Japanese AMA.

2   Abstract of EU Competition Law

The articles from Article 101 to Article 109 of the Treaty of the Functioning of the European Union (hereinafter 'TFEU') sets forth the competition lawrules in the European Community[2]. Among those articles, Article 101 and Article 102 describe the basic principles of the EU Competition Law. Article 101 of TFEU regulates the

---

1.Case T-201/04 *Microsoft Corp v. Commission* [2007] ECR II-3601.

2.*Takigawa* at 155-156.

harmonized conducts made by multiple undertakings, and Article 102 of TFEU governs the sole conducts by single undertaking[3].

The purpose of those articles in the TFEU is to protect not only efficient free competitionbut also the 'workable competition' in the market[4], which will contribute to the EU's general purpose of the integration of the single markets in the European Union territory. The EU Competition Lawholds (a) protection of the market efficiency and free competition as its primary objective and (b) protection of competitors and fair competition as one of its other objectives[5].

3 Cases of Refusal of Trade for Tangible Assets

3-1 Overview

Before considering the cases of refusal of license for IP rights, this section will examine the cases of refusal of trade for tangible assets and confirm the basic principles of the EU Competition Law's regulation. In general, there is no duty for a dominant undertaking to supply its assets to others undertakings[6]. When there exists a special situation, a dominant undertaking's refusal of trade can constitute an abuse of its position[7].

3-2 Cases of Refusal of Trade

The discipline in the refusal of trade cases has been uniquely developed through from the Commercial Solvents case to the recent cases of the Essential Facilitiesdoctrine. It should be noted that the Essential Facilities doctrine involves several special aspects strongly influenced by the EU's general objective of integrating the single market within the EU territory[8].

3-2-1 Commercial Solvents Case

A refusal of trade was clearly recognized as a violation of Article 102 in the Commercial

---

3.See Ezrachi, EU Competition Law, An Analytical Guide to the Leading Cases 262-264 & 592-59 (6th ed. 2018) [hereinafter *Ezrachi 2018*].

4.*Cf.* Case 26/76 *Metro-SB-Grofimarkte GmbH v. Commission* [1977] ECR 1875, [1978] 2 CMLR 1.

5.Jones et al., EU COMPETITION LAW, TEXT, CASES AND MATERIALS 30-31 (7th ed. 2019) [hereinafter *Jones et al.*].

6.*Cf.* Case 27/76 *United Brands v. Commission* [1978] ECR 207 paras 215-219 [hereinafter *United Brands Case*].

7.*Jones et al.* at 484-485. Also *see* Korah, An Introductory Guide to EC Competition Law and Practice 172 (7th ed. 2007) [hereinafter *Korah 2007*].

8.*Jones et al.* at 34.

Solvents case (1974)[9]. In this case, the European Court of Justiceconfirmed Commercial Solvents' refusal to supply a raw material, aminobutanol, to a manufacturer of ethambutol products, Zoja, as an abusive conduct under the EU Competition Law[10]. Zoja was an independent manufacturer, and the aim of Commercial Solvents' refusal of trade was for the anti-competitive purpose of excluding Zoja from the product market. In addition, Commercial Solvents was the only provider of the raw material of ethambutol products at that time, and the production scheme of the raw material was held only by Commercial Solvents[11].

Given the situation above, the European Commission's decision to intervene in the Commercial Solvents' refusal of trade for the raw material was upheld by the court. Commercial Solvents was in the dominant position in this case and refused to supply the raw material in order to restrain competition in the downstream market[12].

3-2-2   United Brands Case

In the United Brands case (1978)[13]it was concluded that a dominant undertaking's conduct of charging excessive and discriminatory price could constitute a violation of Article 102, even if the refusal of trade was in response to a perceived threat in the market[14].

In this case, United Brands refused to supply its bananas by charging a discriminatory price to a distributor, Olsen, in response to a start of Olsen's market promotion for United Brand's competitor. This refusal was held to be an abuse of United Brands' dominant position in the relevant market.

In conclusion, the Court of Justice confirmed that United Brands' reduction in supplies to Olsen should be condemned as a violation of the EU Competition Law. This aggressive intervention by the court was made in order to protect a relatively smaller distributor[15].

3-2-3   Hugin Case

In the Hugin case (1979)[16], a dominant undertaker, Hugin, refused to supply its spare parts to its customer, Liptons, in order to operate a repair service business by itself, and Hugin's claim of objective justification could not be accepted by the European

---

9.Cases 6 and 7/73 *Instituto Chemioterapico Italiano Spa and Commercial Solvents Corp v. EC Commission* [1974] ECR 223, [1974] 1 CMLR 309 [hereinafter*Commercial Solvents Case*].

10.*Id.* at para 25.

11.*Id.* at paras 15-16.

12.*Jones et al.* at 485.

13.*United Brands Case.*

14.*Jones et al.* at 520-521.

15.*Id.* at para 182. Also *see Korah 2007* at 92, *Ezrachi 2018* at 620-621.

16.Case 22/78 *Hugin Kassaregister AB and Hugin Cash Registers Ltd v. Commission* [1979] ECR 1869, [1979] 3 CMLR 345.

Commission[17].

The refusal to supply the spare parts to an existing customer was therefore condemned as a violation of Article 102 of the TFEU, although the existing customer could have avoided the refusal of supply if it had entered into a long-term supply contract with Hugin[18]. The Court of Justice also confirmed the dominant position of Hugin condemned by the commission.

3-3   Cases of the Essential Facilities Doctrine

3-3-1   Overview

The European Commissionand the Court of Justice found in the above-mentioned cases that abuse of dominant positionunder Article 102 of TFEU can be constituted by refusal of trade in the market. This understanding of those refusal of trade cases has been further developed as a doctrine of 'essential facilities' (hereinafter 'Essential Facilities doctrine'), i.e., the facilities 'owned or controlled by a vertically integrated dominant undertaking to which other undertakings need access in order to provide products or services to customers' [19]. Also, it should be noted on the Essential Facilities doctrine that a) the doctrine will provide an obligation of supplying access to the facility to new customers as well as existing customers, and b) this doctrine should be mainly discussed in relation to liberalized sectors and transport infrastructures[20].

The Essential Facilitiesdoctrine under the EU Competition Lawhas been discussed in relation to multiple European Commission's decisions. While some early cases did not clearly mention the terminology of 'essential facilities' , the scholars indicate that the doctrine has been employed[21]since the London European Sabena case (1988)[22]and the British-Midland/Aer Lingus case (1992)[23]. The B&I Line/Sealink case (1992)[24]should also be categorized as a case employing the Essential Facilitiesdoctrine. The European Commission concluded that an obligation for providing non-discriminatory access to their competitors should be put upon an owner of the subject facility.

In addition, the Sea Containers Ltd/ Stena case (1993)[25]indicated that Stena Sealink's

---

17.*Jones et al.*at 487.

18.*Korah 2007* at 175, *Ezrachi 2018* at 621.

19.*Jones et al.*at 487-488.

20.*Id.* at 488.

21.*Jones et al.* at 488.

22.*London European-Sabena* [1988] OJL 317/47, [1989] 4 CMLR 662.

23.*British-Midland/Aer Lingus* [1992] OJL 96/34, [1993] 4 CMLR 596.

24.*Sealink/B&I Holyhead: Interim Measures* [1992] 5 CMLR 255 [hereinafter *B&I Case*].

25.*Sea Containers Ltd. v. Stena Sealink Ports* [1994] OJL15/8, [1995] 4 CMLR 84 [hereinafter *Sea Containers Case*].

refusal to grant access to its facility to another undertaking can constitute an abuse of a dominant position. Furthermore, in this case, it became clear that a refusal to supply access not only to existing customers but also new customers can be condemned as an abuse of dominant position. Following this judgement, the Rodby Port case(1993)[26]also maintained the same conclusion in its judgement.

There is still disagreement about the definition of what an essential facility is. Firstly, it is necessary, to be considered as an essential facility, that 'a facility or infrastructure without the access to which competitors cannot provide services to their customers'. Secondly, it is also required that 'access to the facility is not merely desirable for other undertakings but genuinely essential'[27].

Those elements in the above are a basic understanding in the B&I Line/Sealink case of what an essential facility is. However, there exist discussions on whether a definition of the essential facility which has been uniquely developed in the cases of liberalized sectors or transport infrastructures should be maintained in cases of other sectors as it is.

3-3-2   B&I Case (1992)

The B&I case (1992) is recognized as one of the early cases in which the Essential Facilitiesdoctrine was applied to a refusal of trade by the owner of a facility (Sealink). A characteristic of this case is that any unfavourable result in competition was not a primary intention of Sealink, but a consequence of Sealink's conduct[28]. Also, this was a case of refusal to an existing customer[29].

However, on the other hand, we should examine whether its exceptionally narrow definition of a relevant market confirmed by the European Commission, in this case, is a proper approach. The relevant market, in this case, was defined as per the Holyhead port[30].

3-3-3   Sea Containers Case (1993)

In addition, the Sea Containers' decision established that a refusal of non-discriminatory offer of access to a fundamental facility, which is essential for provision of service by other undertakings in the market, can constitute an abuse of a dominant position. We should remark in this case that Sealink was in the unique status of double monopoly

---

26.*Port of Rodby* [1994] OJL55/52, [1994] 5 CMLR 457. [hereinafter *Port of Rodby Case*].

27.*See B&I Case* at paras 61-65.

28.*Id.* para 41-44. *See Ezrachi 2018* at 762.

29.*Jones et al.* at.488-489.

30.*B&I Case* at paras 36-40.

where it controlled both the essential port facility and also maintained a dominant position in the downstream market[31], and this was a case of refusal to a new customer as opposed to an existing customer[32].

However, it should be noted, as well as the B&I case, that the relevant market was narrowly defined[33]. Thus, it is questionable whether this market definition was in accordance with a traditional criterion of the relevant market's definition employed in other cases.

3-3-4   Rodby Case (1993)

In the Rodby case, an undertaking, Euro-Port A/S, tried to newly enter a dominated route, and the Essential Facilitiesdoctrine was applied to a refusal by the Danish government authority[34].

It is notable that the European Commissiondid not approve a claim that a grant of access to the new entrant could jeopardize expansion of the business operated by existing users of the port of Rodby. Furthermore, the commission clarified that a right of expanding the business is not guaranteed unless the use of facility contract explicitly designates such a right[35].

Also, a definition of the relevant market, i.e., the Rodby port itself, in this case[36]was an exceptionally narrower definition than a traditional criterion of the relevant market.

3-3-5   Analysis and Scholar's Opinions

As confirmed in the above, while the cases of the Essential Facilitiesdoctrine can be categorized as a kind of a refusal of trade case, we can find several elements which go beyond a traditional approach[37].

Firstly, we can observe a set of characteristics from those decisions in the above that those property owners maintain their dominant position regarding transport infrastructures or liberalized sectors.

Secondly, as a basic requirement of regulation under the Essential Facilitiesdoctrine, an owner of a facility must maintain a dominant position in the upstream market. Although the facility owner's dominant position in both the upstream market and the downstream

---

31.*Sea Containers Case* at paras 75-76.

32.*Id.* at para 67. *See Jones et al.* at 488-489.

33.*Sea Containers Case* at paras 61-65.

34.*Port of Rodby Case* at para 12.

35.*Id.* at paras 14-16.

36.*Id.* at paras 7-9.

37.Lang, *Competition Law and Regulation Law from an EC Perspectives*, 23 Fordham International Law Journal 116, 117 (2000) [hereinafter *Lang 2000*],*available at* https://ir.lawnet.fordham.edu/cgi/viewcontent.cgi?article=1715&context=ilj.

market is not required, the requirement of access to the facility becomes stronger than in other cases if an owner of the facility is in a dominant position in both markets[38].

Lastly, a market definition is more narrowly defined than the traditional criterion under EU Competition Law[39]. Scholarly opinion suggests that the demand for price elasticity with respect to alternative services should have been used for the definition of the relevant market. However, in those cases, it was unclear whether the elasticity to alternative transportation routes was precisely analyzed. We can presume that the EU Competition Law's objectives of the achievement of an integrated market and the free movement of goods might drive this exceptional market definition.

On the other hand, it is recommendable, in view of a microeconomics analysis, that the Essential Facilitiesdoctrine should be cautiously applied. A grant of access to private property does not bring an economically favourable result.

Aggressive application of the Essential Facilities doctrine can lead to the undertaking's disincentive for future investment[40]. Only in exceptional circumstances will an order of granting access to the facilities improve a benefit to consumers in the market. An exceptionally narrow definition of the relevant market under the Essential Facilitiesdoctrine should be more carefully reexamined.

3-3-6. Summary

Why did the European Commissionemploy the exceptionally narrow definition of the relevant market and force an obligation of granting a non-discriminatory access of the facilities on the owner? It is the author's understanding that a consideration of the European social-political reasoning, i.e., the EU's general objective of integrating the single market within the EU territory[41], that has influenced the application of the Essential Facilitiesdoctrine in those cases. In accordance with this understanding, the Essential Facilities doctrine has been applied to the cases of transport infrastructures or liberalized sectors within the EU territory[42].

If this author's understanding is correct, a discussion on possible application of the Essential Facilities doctrine under the Japanese AMA to the cases in other sectors, such as standard technology in the IT industry, would not be reasonable.

38.See Lang, *Defining Legitimate Competition: Company' s Duties to Supply Competition and Access to Essential Facilities*, 18 Fordham International Law Journal 437, 477-478 (1994) (hereinafter *Lang 1994*), *available at* https://ir.lawnet.fordham.edu/cgi/viewcontent.cgi?article=1411&context=ilj.

39.Fujiwara, *Oushu ni okeru essenshal facility ron no keiju - part 2 [Inheritance of the essential facilities doctrine in the Europe-part 2]* 74-3 Hougaku-kenkyu 37, 50 (2001). See also Ridyard, *Essential Facilities and the Obligation to Supply Competitors under UK and EC Competition Law* 8 European Competition Law Review 438, 442-443 (1996) [hereinafter *Ridyard*].

40.Bishop, *Essential Facilities: The Rising Tide*, 4 European Competition Law Review 183, 183 (1998) [hereinafter *Bishop*].

41.*Jones et al.* at 34.

42.*See Lang 1994* at 439-440.

3-4 Conclusion

The EU Competition Lawhas a characteristic in its positive application of the Essential Facilitiesdoctrine. However, we should note that the doctrine involves an exceptionally narrow market definition and an obligation of granting non-discriminatory access. The author believes that this exceptional approach would be justified by the EU Competition Law's unique objectives. This means that in the Japanese AMA the Japanese authorities should be very cautious in applying the Essential Facilities doctrine to the cases of other sectors than the sector of transport infrastructures or liberalized sectors.

The following chapter will examine how the European authorities have approached the cases of refusal of license for IP rights, where the EU's objective of the single market integration is less important, and consideration for the incentive of technology development is more important.

4 Cases of Refusal of License for IP Rights

4-1 Overview

Following an analysis of the cases of refusal of trade for tangible assets, this chapter will analyze the unique criteria in the refusal of license for IP rights cases. The Exceptional Circumstances test was employed in the cases of refusal of license for IP rights in the Magill case (1995). However, It should be remarked that the Exceptional Circumstances test has been transformed through the Microsoftcase (2007) and the European Commission's guidance.

4-2 Details of Cases

4-2-1 AB Volvo Case

In the AB Volvo case (1988)[43]it was held by the European Court of Justicethat, while it was not illegal per se to refuse to grant a license for the design rights on its car parts, in special circumstances it can constitute a violation of the EU Competition Law. More precisely, the court indicated that the refusal should be deemed as a violation of Article 102 of the TFEU under the situation where a 'certain abusive conduct' was involved. We should note that any broad obligation, such as the obligation under the Essential Facilitiesdoctrine, was not discussed in this case[44]. The Court of Justice indicated that only in those cases where the refusal is 'arbitrary', the refusal to provide those spare

---

43.Case 238/87 *AB Volvo v. Erik Veng* [1988] ECR 6211, [1989] 4 CMLR 122 [hereinafter *AB Volvo Case*].
44.*See Jones et al.* at 503-504,*Korah 2007*at 176.

parts can breach Article 102.

4-2-2 Magill Case

In the Magill case (1995)[45]a refusal of license for the copyrightsof television program schedules was argued. There was a unique situation in the UK and Ireland where a compilation of information, such as television program schedules, could be protected by the copyrights law.

The ECJ indicates in this case that refusal of license can constitute a violation of Article 102 only in 'Exceptional Circumstances'. More specifically, the 'Exceptional Circumstances' in the Magill case meant that a) there existed 'no substitute' for a weekly guide, b) creation of a 'new product' in the market was blocked by the refusal, c) 'no justification' for the refusal was confirmed, and d) competition in the secondary market was 'hampered' by the refusal[46]. Among those criteria, as stated in the following, the requirement of 'a) no substitute' and 'b) new product' can constitute especially important criteria in view of a balance between protection of market competition and promotion of technological innovation.

Furthermore, it should be noted that a terminology of 'refusal to supply raw material', rather than 'essential facility' or 'the Essential Facilitiesdoctrine', was carefully used by the ECJ in this case. Also, the court clarified that the refusal of license does not constitute a violation of Article 102 in an ordinary situation[47].

In addition, we should remember that this case involved statutory monopolists, who were granted their license by the government authorities. This means that there was no strong need for careful consideration for negative influence on future incentive to investment in the market which can be caused by the intervention by Competition Law. Since those dominant positions held by the copyrightsowners had been established by the statutory regulation rather than their own investment effort in the market.

Moreover, attention should be paid to the fact that their copyrighted materials, the program listings, were uniquely protected under the UK law and Irish law. The creativity of the program listing was unclear, and its protection under the CopyrightsLaw in other countries was questionable[48]. This also suggests that there was no strong need for consideration of disincentive to future creation caused by the Competition Law's intervention.

45.Cases C-241-242/91 *PRTE & ITP v. Commission*[1995] ECR I-743 [hereinafter*Magill Case*].

46.*Magill Case* at paras 53-56.

47.*Jones et al.* at 504-506. *See Ezrachi 2018*at 727-729

48.*See Korah 2007* at 177.

In summary, in light of those special factors, in this case, the author concludes that those criteria held in the Magill case should not be generalized in other refusal of license cases. Those criteria are carefully prepared for the unique situation. The over-generalization of those criteria will lead to a serious negative influence on future incentive to prospective IP rights owners. In particular, if it is a case of refusal of license for patents, this concern should be especially emphasized in view of a proper balance between the protection of market competition and the promotion of technological innovation. The criteria of Competition Law's intervention should be individually examined in accordance with the category of subject IP rights, such as patents, copyrights, trade secrets or other rights, in each case[49].

4-2-3   IMS Case

Refusal to provide a data system including pharmaceuticalsales data, which incorporated information regarding postcodes, administrative boundaries and the details of doctors and pharmacies in Germany, was discussed in the IMS case (2004)[50]. Other undertakings could not duplicate this data system due to the regulation of German privacy law.

In response to an enquiry from the German court, the ECJ clarified[51] the criteria for an abusive refusal of license for copyrights. The ECJ stated the following cumulative criteria: a) the refusal is blocking the emergence of 'new product' , b) provision of the protected material is 'indispensable' , c) competition in the downstream market would be 'excluded' by the refusal, and d) there exists 'no justification' for the refusal[52]. This meant that Competition Law's intervention could only be allowed in the 'Exceptional Circumstances' which was coming from the Magill case.

In the judgement of IMS case, it should also be emphasized that the data system

---

49. We should also note the Oscar Bronner case (1998) [Case C-7/97 *Oscar Bronner GmbH and Co KG v. Mediaprint Zeitungs und Zeitschriftenverlag GmbH and Co KG* [1998] ECR I-7791] which is a leading case clarifying the requirement of limited circumstances, while it is not a case of refusal of license for IP rights. Following the Magill case(1995), the Oscar Bronner case expressed the strict requirement for application of the essential facility doctrine, from a view that the protection of consumers, rather than competitors, is a main concern of Article 102. The four requirements in this case for infringement of Article 102 in refusal to supply case were clarified as follows: a) the refusal is likely to eliminate all competition in the downstream market, b) the refusal does not involve objective justification, c) the access is indispensable fir other undertaking' s business, and d) there is no substitute or possible substitute. The ECJ declared that the refusal of access did not eliminate all competition but made harder in competition, and the access was just viable for the other undertaking rather than indispensable. Accordingly, the court held that the refusal in this case did not satisfy those requirements in the above. In other words, it confirmed that limited circumstances must exist for imposing the obligation of granting access to an owner of facility.

50. Case C-418/01 *IMS Health GmbH & Co. OHG v. NDC Health GmbH & Co. KG* [2004] ECR I-5039, [2004] 4 CMLR 1543 [hereinafter *IMS Case*].

51. *NDC Health/IMS: Interim Measures* [2004] OJL59/18, [2002] 4 CMLR 111.

52. *IMS Case* at para 37.

constituting a de-facto standard in the market and protected by copyrightsunder the German law was argued in this case. Scholar's opinions have pointed out that protection of the data system was granted by a peculiarity of the Copyrights Law of Germany[53]. In other words, the criterion of Competition Law's intervention in the IMS case should not be generalized to the cases of refusal of license for other IP rights.

In addition, in terms of the criterion of 'b) indispensability', we should note that the competitor of IMS succeeded in obtaining alternative material to the data system, and thus the interim decision was withdrawn[54]. Moreover, the information contained in the data system was incidentally created as a result of IMS's routine business activities, rather than a special development work for the creation of the data system. This means that there was no particularly strong need for consideration on negative influence to future incentive to creation which will be caused by the Competition Law's intervention in this case.

Accordingly, over-generalization of the criteria should be avoided, especially in relation to the cases where a refusal of license involves other categories of IP rights, such as patents. This means that those criteria should be individually examined in accordance with the category of subject IP rights, as well as the category of subject standard, i.e., de-facto or de-jure, in each case.

4-2-4   Microsoft Case

Refusal to provide interface information, which was necessary for maintaining software's 'interoperability' among systems and programs, was argued in the Microsoftcase (2007)[55]. When a dominant position in the upstream market is maintained by the company, the refusal to provide the interface information can restrain competition in the downstream market and constitute a violation of Article 102 of TFEU.

In this case the European Commissionordered that Microsoftmust provide the interface information required for maintaining the interoperability to other undertakings competing in the market of workgroup server operating systems (hereinafter 'WGOS') and periodically update that information. One difference from the Magill case here was that the refusal of supply was conducted against existing partners rather than new partners. Under this situation, the European Commissionjudged that Microsoft's refusal constitutes an abuse of dominant positionunder Article 102[56].

53.*Jones et al.*at 509. *See Ezrachi 2018* at 733-734.

54.Commission Decision 2003/741/EC, 13 Aug. 2003, [2003] OJL268/69; IP03/1159.

55.Case T-201/04 *Microsoft v. EC Commission* [2007] ECRII-3601 [hereinafter*Microsoft Case*].

56.*Id.* at paras 316-317.

In terms with this judgement, we should note that the 'indispensability' of the interface information was properly examined through considering: a) necessity of the interoperability between WGOS products and Windows PC operating systems for viable competition in the market, and b) indispensability of the interface information for maintaining the interoperability among the relevant products[57].

On the other hand, this judgement employed a more elastic criterion than the original criterion held in the IMS case. In this respect, the European Commissionpointed out the following uniqueness of the Microsoftcase: a) the interface information which Microsoft refused to supply was necessary for maintaining the interoperability, b) extraordinary power in the market was held by Microsoft, and c) its supply was refused to existing partners rather than new partners[58]. This commission's elastic understanding was also supported by the Court of Justice.

More precisely, the original criteria in the IMS case were relaxed in several aspects in this Microsoft case as follows.

(1) 'New Product'

It should be emphasized that due to the uniqueness of the Microsoftcase the European Commissionrevised the criterion of 'a) blocking appearance of new product' . The commission alternatively required the criterion of 'limiting technical development' which covers both follow-on innovation and break-through innovation. This means that the criterion held in the IMS case was largely relaxed, and this will allow for a more aggressive Completion Law's intervention in a refusal of license situation. In other words, even if the situation does not block the appearance of a new product, a refusal of license can constitute a violation of Article 102 of TFEU.

Furthermore, in terms of the criterion of 'new product' , the European Court clearly held that the circumstances 'cannot be the only parameter which determines whether a refusal to license an intellectual property right is capable of causing prejudice to consumers within the meaning of Article 82 (b) EC. As that provision states, such prejudice may arise where there is a limitation not only of production on markets, but also of technical development' [59]. This clearly means that the court's judgement widened the criterion from 'blocking appearance of new product' to 'limiting technical development' , and the threshold of the Competition Law's intervention was thus largely

---

57.*Id.* at para 658. *See Jones et al.* at 510-511.

58.*Id.* at paras 316-317. *See Jones et al.* at 512, *Korah 2007* at 185-186.

59.*Id.* at para 647. *See* Ezrachi, *Competition Law Enforcement and Refusal to Licence - The Changing Boundaries of Article 102 TFEU, in* Intellectual Property and Competition Law: New Frontiers 95, 98-99 (Anderman & Ezrachi eds, 2011) [hereinafter *Ezrachi 2011*], *Jones et al.* at 517, *Ezrachi 2018* at 742-743.

relaxed from the judgement in IMS case.

(2) 'Indispensability'

Regarding another criterion of 'b) indispensability' in the IMS case, the Microsoftcase confirmed its principle that the criterion of 'indispensability' should be maintained as one of its criteria.

However, we should note a fact in this case that, although competitor's products were compatible with the Windows operating system without using the interface information, the competitor's products incorporating the interface information could work more efficiently. This means that the European court changed its understanding of the 'indispensability' criterion from 'essential' for market activity to 'convenient' for market activity[60]. More precisely, the IMS case regarded the 'absence of a potential or actual substitute' situation as the 'indispensable' status. However, the court in the Microsoftcase alternatively deemed the 'economically indispensable' situation, where elimination of economic viability caused by the provision of a potential or actual substitute can be expected, as the 'indispensable' status[61].

(3) 'Elimination of All Competition'

In terms of the criterion of 'c) elimination of all competition' in the secondary market, the Microsoftcase indicated that the 'elimination of all effective competition' in the market can satisfy this criterion. This should be regarded as another elastic interpretation of the original criteria held in the IMS case[62].

In more details, the Microsoft case clearly stated that it was not 'necessary to demonstrate that all competition on the market would be eliminated. What matters, for the purpose of establishing an infringement of Article 82 EC, is that the refusal at issue is liable to, or is likely to, eliminate all effective competition on the market'[63]. The Microsoftcase relaxed the criterion from the elimination of 'all competition' to 'all effective competition' in the market. This means that, even if there exists 'a marginal presence in certain niches on the market'[64], this criterion can be fulfilled by the dominant undertaker's refusal.

As we can see above, the Microsoft case made it possible to employ the more relaxed

---

60.*Id.* at para 237.

61.Andreangeli, *Interoperability as an essential facility in the Microsoft case–encouraging competition or stifling innovation?*, 34(4) European Law Review 584, 597-598 (2009) [hereinafter *Andreangeli 2009*], Ridyard, *Compulsory Access under EC Competition Law – A New Doctrine of "Convenient Facilities" and the Case for Price Regulation,*25 European Competition Law Review 669, 670 (2004) [hereinafter*Ridyard 2004*], *Jones et al.* at 516-517, *Ezrachi 2018* at 741.

62.*Microsoft Case*at para 563.*SeeJones et al.* at 517,*Ezrachi 2018*at 741-742,*Korah 2007*at 186,*Ezrachi 2011*at 99.

63.*Id.*

64.*Id.*

criteria for the competition law's intervention in the refusal of license. However, it should be carefully noted that this elastic criterion was accepted under the unique situation in the Microsoft case which involves information for securing the 'interoperability' and the strong 'network effects' among PC and server users in the market.

(4) 'Efficiency defence'

In the Microsoftcase, it was shown that it is difficult for a dominant undertaking to insist on the 'efficiency defence' in the court. In fact, the European court did not accept Microsoft's plea of serious disincentive to technological innovation in the market, and it indicated that Microsoft's argument was too vague and theoretical to employ in its judgement.

However, this decision as to the merits of the efficiency argument in this case is contestable. The court should have more precisely evaluated a balance between the negative effect to market competition caused by the dominant undertaking's refusal to disclose the interface information and another negative effect on incentive to innovation caused by compulsory disclosure of the information in the market. In this regard, we should remark that the Microsoftcase showed how the efficiency improvement in the market should be evaluated. Especially, the court's interpretation of the improvement of efficiency caused by long-term innovation and short/middle-term innovation is worthy of note.

In addition, this case clarified that a burden of proof in the efficiency defence lay with the dominant undertaker, although a dominant position and the exceptional circumstances must be proved by the European Commission[65]. Based on this understanding, a dominant undertaker should carefully confirm whether it is possible to prove the whole efficiency improvement which is mainly promoted by break-through innovation of new innovative technology as opposed to follow-on innovation of improvements for existing technology.

In terms with the efficiency defence, as shown in the Microsoftcase, it is difficult for a dominant undertaking to establish that its incentive to innovate outweighs improvement of innovation in the whole industry through 'specifying the technologies or products to which it thus referred'[66] and showing numerical analysis in the whole industry, especially in the new economy such as IT industry, which relies mainly on the break-through innovation of new innovative technology. Efficiency improvement brought by break-through innovation has different characteristics from the improvement brought by follow-on innovation, such as daily technological improvements of existing

---

65.*Id.* at par 688.
66.*Id.* at para 698.

technology. It is difficult to compare the two efficiency improvements on the one scale. In other words, the former is the long-term efficiency improvement, and the latter is the short/middle term efficiency improvement. Especially when it involves a refusal of license in the new market, the comparison between the two different efficiencies is a difficult requirement for a dominant undertaking.

Besides, if we focus on future negative influence to the break-through innovation by other innovators, the comparison would become more complicated. It will be more difficult to accurately evaluate the improvement of efficiency. Even though the importance of incentives to the long-term innovation is obvious, especially in the new market, there remain difficulties to prove a numerical comparison between the effect in the follow-on innovation in the short/mid-term and the break-through innovation in the long-term. The different natures of those two forms of innovation will cause many difficulties in the comparison.

(5) Summary

In summary, as far as a burden of proof being placed upon a dominant undertaker, it would be difficult for the dominant undertaking to prove improvement of efficiency, unless there will be the change of burden from a dominant undertaking to the authority. Accordingly, the dominant undertaking would focus on how it can prove the other criteria in the 'Exceptional Circumstances' test.

Thus, it is the author's opinion that the importance of maintaining the original criteria of the 'Exceptional Circumstances' test in the IMS case should be emphasized for protecting incentive to technological innovation by the leading innovators especially in the new market, such as IT industry, where the break-through innovation tends to play a more important role than the follow-on innovation. Also, in those cases involving the other categories of IP rights such as patents or copyrights, where the incentive to technology development work by inventors or creators should be more carefully protected, the original criteria in the IMS case should be maintained.

In other words, it is difficult to maintain those incentives to technological innovation, if prospective IP rights owners must rely on the elastic criteria provided in the Microsoftcase and the 'efficiency defence' placing a burden of proof on the IP right owners.

Again, we should pay attention to the special factors in the Microsoft case such as the refusal of supply of information for securing 'interoperability' , the existence of 'network effects' among users in the market, and the improvement of the total innovation in the software market. The elastic criteria were thus introduced on the delicate balance in the unique Microsoftsituation among a) the risk of the negative effect to market competition reinforced by reliance on 'interoperability' and influence of 'network effects' , b) disincentive to the individual innovation supported by Microsoft, and c) improvement of the total innovation promoted by the other innovators in the whole market.

It is not appropriate to generalize its elastic criteria as the common standard for the Competition Law's intervention in every refusal of license situation. The court and authority should properly recognize that the Microsoft case was one extreme situation in the refusal of license situation. The author is concerned that such generalization of the elastic criteria can impair future incentive to technological innovation and lead to an excessive interventionist approach.

4-2-5 After the Microsoft Case: Clearstream Case (2009)

In the Clearstream case[67]the Clearstream Banking AG and its parent company Clearstream International SA (hereinafter 'Clearstream'), which provide financial services, refused to supply data access necessary for maintaining 'interoperability' of the securities clearing and settlement services to their competitor, Euroclear Bank SA. Consequently, former customers of Euroclear Bank SA had no choice but to use those services provided by Clearstream. The European Commissionidentified in this case that Clearstream's refusal to supply the subject data and its offering of discriminatory prices for them constituted a violation of Article 102.

In this case we should remark that the European Commission confirmed that the refusal to supply the data access could impair the future innovation in the market. In addition, it should also be noted that the court supported the commission's decision based on the elastic criteria held in the Microsoftcase[68].
However, attention should be paid to a fact that this Clearstream case involved a refusal of data access to new entrants in the financial service market. The author believes that, if this is a case of refusal of license for patents or copyrights, the court's judgement on the elastic criteria held in the Microsoft case may be different. We should note that negative effects on the future technological innovation caused by the Competition Law's intervention can become more serious in the cases of patents or copyrights than the cases of data or information.

4-2-6 Summary

As examined above, the original criteria of the 'Exceptional Circumstances' test for refusal of license for IP rights were established in the Magill case and IMS case.

67.Case T-301/04 *Clearstream Banking AG v. Commission*, 9 September 2009 [hereinafter*Clearstream Case*].

68.*Clearstream Case* at paras 146-147, *Jones et al.* at 500, *Ezrachi 2018* at 756-757.

Following these cases, in the Microsoftcase, those criteria were revised toward more elastic criteria for refusal of supplying interface information. Also, the Clearstream case approved these elastic criteria for a refusal of providing data access. However, it is still not clear how the European court and authority will apply the elastic criteria held in the Microsoft case and Clearstream case to the cases of refusal of license for other categories of IP rights, such as patents or copyrights.

In this regards, the next chapter will examine details of the elastic criteria in the European Commission's guidance and explain how the commission's guidelines are following this elastic approach.

4-3 EC Guidance Paper

In addition to the case analysis in the above, it is also necessary to examine details of the European Commission's (hereinafter 'EC') guidance on refusal of license for IP rights.

It should be noted that after a judgement in the Microsoft case (2007), the commission's Guidance Paper (hereinafter 'Guidance Paper')[69]was announced in 2009. The Guidance Paper provides its own criteria for the refusal of license situation which incorporates multiple differences from the original criteria established in the IMS case (2004).

4-3-1 'New Product'

Firstly, the Guidance Paper relaxed the criterion of 'appearance of a new product' in accordance with the understanding of the Microsoftcase. This guidance clearly sets out that 'This may be particularly the case if the undertaking which requests supply does not intend to limit itself essentially to duplicating the goods or services already offered by the dominant undertaking on the downstream market, but intends to produce new or improved goods or services for which there is a potential consumer demand or is likely to contribute to technical development' [70].

Based on this statement mentioning 'new or improved goods or services' , we can observe that the European Commissionfollowed the court's elastic criterion in the Microsoftcase, i.e., 'limitation of technical development' , as opposed to the original criterion of 'blocking appearance of a new product' in the IMS case.

However, we should note that the Microsoftcase was about a refusal of license to existing

---

69.Communication from the Commission, Guidance on the Commission's enforcement priorities in applying Article 82 of the EC Treaty to abusive exclusionary conduct by dominant undertakings [2009] OJC 45/2 [hereinafter *Guidance Paper*], *available at* https://eur-lex.europa.eu/legal-content/EN/TXT/HTML/?uri=CELEX:52009XC0224(01)&from=EN.

70.*Guidance Paper* at para 87. *See Andreangeli 2009* at 608, *Jones et al.* at 522-523, *Ezrachi 2018* at 747.

partners, rather than new partners, which involved a block of 'interoperability' and a lock-insituation caused by strong 'network effects'. An anti-competitive effect caused by the refusal could be thus clearly observed. Considering this characteristic of the Microsoft case, we should be cautious to generalize the criterion of 'limitation of technical development'. It would not be appropriate to regard this criterion as the general criterion for judgement in refusal of license for IP rights cases.

4-3-2 'Elimination of Competition'

Secondly, the European Commissionalso followed the elastic criterion of 'elimination of all effective competition', as opposed to 'elimination of all competition', held in the Microsoftcase. Moreover, it insists on the use of the market structure approach, rather than the economic effect approach, in order to evaluate foreclosures of the market. In this regard, the Guidance Paper explicitly states that 'if the conduct has been in place for a sufficient period of time, the market performance of the dominant undertaking and its competitors may provide direct evidence of anti-competitive foreclosure. For reasons attributable to the allegedly abusive conduct, the market share of the dominant undertaking may have risen or a decline in market share may have been slowed'[71].

We should remark that, although the Guidance Paper, on the one hand, regards the effect of consumer harm as the most important factor and thus indicates that the commission's analysis should be conducted based on the effects-oriented approach, the guidance seeks, on the other hand, to maintain the market structure approach.

The author believes that the effects-oriented approach should have been more clearly emphasized in the guidance for judgement of 'elimination of all competition'.

4-3-3 'Indispensability'

In the Guidance Paper, the criterion of 'indispensability' was discussed as an 'objective necessity' which requires the situation that there exists no actual or potential substitute to counter negative consequences of the refusal. However, this understanding shows a clear contrast to that in the Bronner case (1998)[72]. The Bronner case clearly expressed its strict requirement for intervention in a refusal of trade situation. In the Bronner case, the European court expressed that the refusal of access did not eliminate all competition but made competition harder, and the access was just viable for other undertakings rather than indispensable. In other words, the court confirmed that genuine 'indispensability' of refused material, rather than just 'viability', must exist in refusal of trade cases[73].

71.*Guidance Paper* at para 85. *See Andreangeli 2009* at 607-608, *Jones et al.* at 522.

72.Case C-7/97 *Oscar Bronner GmbH and Co KG v. Mediaprint Zeitungs und Zeitschriftenverlag GmbH and Co KG* [1998] ECR I-7791.

73.*Id.* paras 41-46.

It is the author's opinion that the Guidance Paper's 'liberal' understanding was influenced by the approach of 'economic indispensability' held in the Microsoftcase[74]. However, it should be noted that, as mentioned in the previous chapter, the notion of 'economic indispensability' was introduced in order to recover the competition in the market under the special Microsoft situation involving a block of 'interoperability' and a lock-insituation caused by strong 'network effects'.

Apart from the extreme situation of the Microsoft case, we should discuss whether the unique criterion of 'economic indispensability' in the Microsoft case should be generalized in the Guidance Paper. It is necessary to pay careful attention to the negative effect on technological innovation and the dynamic efficiency which can be caused by its generalization. The author believes that the European Commissionshould have maintained the strict original criterion of 'indispensability' held in the Bronner case in order to avoid possible negative influence on future incentive to technology development.

4-3-4 'Efficiency defence'

Finally, the Guidance Paper states that the 'efficiency defence'[75]can be established by a dominant undertaking. This defence allows the exemption from violation in the following occasions: there exists a) a need of the dominant undertaking's adequate return on its investment, or b) negative effect to the innovation and disincentive for a dominant undertaking to invest in the future R&D[76].

More precisely, it is supported in the guidance that the following elements shown in the European Commission's Discussion Paper in 2005[77]should be fulfilled for establishing the 'efficiency defence'. The elements are as follows: a) efficiencies are realized or likely to be realized as a result of the conduct concerned, b) efficiencies are caused by the conduct, and the conduct is indispensable to the realization of efficiencies, c) efficiencies are beneficial to consumers, and d) competition in respect to a substantial part of the products is not eliminated[78].

4-4 Summary

In summary, we can observe from the Guidance Paper that its understanding of the

---

74.*Guidance Paper* at para 83. *See Andreangeli 2009* at 607, *Jones et al.* at 522, *Cf. Ezrachi 2018* at 747.

75.*Guidance Paper* at para 89.

76.*See Andreangeli 2009* at 608-609, *Jones et al.* at 522, *Ezrachi 2018* at 609-611.

77.DG Competition discussion paper on the application of Article 82 of the Treaty to exclusionary abuses (Dec. 2005) [2005] para 84, *available at* http://ec.europa.eu/competition/antitrust/art82/discpaper2005.pdf.

78.*Andreangeli 2009* at 608-609, *Ezrachi 2018* at 609-611.

criteria for the 'Exceptional Circumstances' test is largely influenced by the judgement of the Microsoftcase. Consequently, the guidance's criteria incorporate substantial differences from the original criteria held in the IMS case.

The generalization of such relaxed criteria shown in the Guidance Paper, apart from the unique factual details in the Microsoft case, i.e., 'interoperability' and 'network effects' , will bring a negative influence to future incentive to technology development. Especially, the relaxation in guidance's criteria of 'elimination of all effective competition' and 'objective necessity' can cause a serious risk.

Accordingly, the author believes that the European Commissionshould carefully reconsider their generalization of its relaxed criteria in the 'Exceptional Circumstances' test. Especially in terms of the cases of refusal of license for patents, careful assessment should be required for maintaining an appropriate balance between the protection of market competition and the promotion of technological innovation.

Following the above-mentioned discussions of the policy-making for restriction on refusal of license for IP rights, the restriction on refusal of license for standard essential patent, involving a FRANDlicense commitment, has been recently developed in Europe[79]. Also, in response to this European trend, the authorities in East Asian countries have incorporated the European approach into their legal system. The next chapter will introduce those current moves on the restriction on refusal of license for standard essential patents in the East Asian countries and the EU jurisdiction.

79.It should be noted that an European scholarly opinion insists that Huawei v. ZTE (2015) case should have maintained the 'exceptional circumstances' test, which has been employed in the refusal of license cases, as apposed to newly employing the 'willing prospective licensee' test. The author believes that an integrated 'exceptional circumstances' test combining 'exceptional circumstances' test and 'willing prospective licensee' test should be one option to be examined for the situation involving standard essential patents. See Goikoetxea, *Huawei v ZTE should have been treated as a refusal to contract - to grant SEP licences - and not as a new category of abuse*, 40(2) European Competition Law Review 67, (2019) [hereinafter *Goikoetxea 2019*].

Chapter 4

SEP Enforcement :
Samsung's SEP Cases
in Japan and Europe

1　Situation in Japan

1-1　Overview: Article 21 of the AMA

In Japan, as mentioned in the above, the proper IP rights enforcement is exempted from the regulation of Anti-Monopoly Act ('AMA'), and other forms of IP rights enforcement beyond the proper enforcement will be subject to the AMA's regulation such as Article 100 (1) of the AMA which may revoke patent rights.

In this regard, the Guidelines for the Use of Intellectual Property under the Anti-Monopoly Act (hereinafter 'IP Guideline') by Japan Fair Trade Commission (hereinafter 'JFTC') provides that those IP enforcement against the IP law system's purpose of promoting inventor's innovation and active utilization of technologies can be regarded as beyond the scope of the proper enforcement of IP[1]. The IP Guideline insists that the judgement of the scope of the proper enforcement of IP should be carefully made in accordance with the purpose of patents law, trademarklaw, copyrightslaw and other IP laws.

Anti-Monopoly Act

Article 21

The provisions of this Act do not apply to acts found to constitute an exercise of rights under the Copyright Act, Patent Act, Utility Model Act, Design Act or Trademark Act.

The Intellectual Property Basic Act of Japan (2003) reconfirms the IP Guideline's understanding in its Article 10. Article 10 clarifies that protection of IP rights shall be subject to restrictions for the security of fair and free competitionas follows.

Intellectual Property Basic Act

Article 10 (Consideration for promoting competition)

In promoting measures for the creation, protection and exploitation of intellectual property, consideration shall be paid to secure the fair exploitation of intellectual property and public interests and to promote fair and free competition.

1-2　Apple vs. Samsung Case by the IP High Court (2014)

The Japanese IP High Courtmade its judgement in 2014 on the standard essential patent (hereinafter 'SEP') disputes for mobile telecommunication technology between

---

1.*See JFTC IP Guideline* at Section 1-1.

Samsung Electronics and Apple Japan[2], which was later incorporated as the legal framework of the restriction of SEP enforcement in the JFTC's IP Guideline and the JPO's SEP Licensing Negotiations Guide.

In this Apple vs. Samsung case (2014) Samsung's enforcement of SEP for Universal Mobile Telecommunications System (UMTS) technology formally standardized in a standard setting organization (SSO), European Telecommunications Standards Institute (ETSI), was argued in the IP High Court. In the course of the standardization process, the ETSIhad obligated its member parties to disclose all their holding patents essential for practising the UMTS technology and make a declaration of granting a license of the SEP under the fair, reasonable and non-discriminatory (hereinafter 'FRAND') terms.

Under these circumstances, Samsung owned its SEP ('898' patent) related to Apple's products (iPhone, iPad2, Wi-Fi+3G, and two other products) implementing the UMTS technology. Although Samsung previously had declared its intention, as a member of the organization, to grant a license of its SEP under the FRANDterms, Samsung filed a lawsuit against Apple claiming injunction and damages based on the infringement of the patent.

In response to Samsung's claim, the IP High Courtindicated that the SEP enforcement of claiming injunction against a willing party hoping to obtain a license under the FRANDterms could prevent the development, manufacturing or sales of products implementing the standard technology and, accordingly, shall constitute the Abuse of Rightsunder Article 1-3 in the Civil Code. Also, the court provided that the claim of the excessive damages, which pursues the amount of damages beyond the reasonable royalty under the FRANDterms, against a willing party hoping to obtain a license under the FRAND terms will not be allowed as a conduct of the Abuse of Rights, unless there exist any special circumstances in the case.

In addition, it was clarified in this case, as mentioned in the above, that the criteria for the judgement of "a willing party hoping to obtain the FRAND terms license" shall consist of the following facts: a) whether the SEP holder indicates a prospective licensee any factual evidence of infringement, b) whether the SEP holder proposes license terms with its reasonable explanation, c) whether a prospective licensee timely responds to the SPE holder's proposal, and d) whether a prospective licensee sincerely negotiates in compliance with the commercial custom.

2.Judgement of IP High Court, 16 Mar. 2014, Heisei 25 (Ne) 10043, Heisei 25 (Ne) 10007, 4, Heisei 25 (Ne) 10008 [hereinafter *Apple v. Samsung Case*].

The author observes that the legal framework of the restriction on SEP enforcement indicated by the IP High Courtshould be regarded as the careful incorporation of the European understanding of the restriction on SEP enforcement prepared by the European Commission, shown in the later-mentioned Samsung and Motorola Mobility cases, into the Japanese legal system. In other words, the common legal understanding of the restriction on SEP enforcement between the European authority and the Japanese court was made by this IP High Court judgement.

1-3   Restriction of IPR Enforcement Related to Technological Standard under AMA

1-3-1   JFTC's IP Guideline under AMA (2007, Revised 2010, 2016)

A framework for the regulation of IP rights enforcement related to technological standard under AMA was provided by the revision of the IP Guideline in 2016 as follows.

JFTC IP Guideline

Part 3 Viewpoints from Private Monopolization and Unreasonable Restraint of Trade

(1) Viewpoints from Private Monopolization

(e) The standard setting organization or trade association (hereinafter referred to as the "SSO") generally makes the document (IPR Policy) describing principles for license of patents (including the other intellectual property rights) essential for implementation of the standards (hereinafter referred to as the "Standard Essential Patent").

[*omitted]

Refusal to license or bringing an action for injunction against a party who is willing to take a license by a FRAND-encumbered Standard Essential Patent holder, or refusal to license or bringing an action for injunction against a party who is willing to take a license by a FRAND-encumbered Standard Essential Patent holder after the withdrawal of the FRAND Declaration for that Standard Essential Patent may fall under the exclusion of business activities of other entrepreneurs by making it difficult to research & develop, produce or sell the products adopting the standards.

The description above shall be applied no matter whether the act is taken by the party which made the FRANDDeclaration or by the party which took over a FRAND-encumbered Standard Essential Patent or is entrusted to manage the FRAND-encumbered Standard Essential Patent. (The same holds for the case described in Part4-(2), (iv).)

[*omitted]

As indicated in the above, JFTCIP Guidelines clarifies that in the event a patent holder of SEP is obliged to declare its will of granting a patent license under the FRANDterms, such SEP enforcement against a willing party by the patent holder can be regarded as an anti-competitive conduct and a violation of the Anti-Monopoly Act. This guidance is prepared for the purpose of avoiding possible prevention of development and utilization of standard technology caused by the abusive SEP enforcement.

1-3-2 Revision of JFTC's IP Guideline and Apple vs. Samsung Case

The above-mentioned revision of JFTCIP Guideline on the SEP enforcement was made in response to the judgement of the Japan IP High Courtin the Apple vs. Samsung case (2014). The judgement firstly provided a basic understanding of civil law regulation under Article 1-3 of the Japan Civil Code against the enforcement of SEP[3].

Having the IP High Court's decision, JFTChad concluded in 2016 that the court's legal framework which restricts the SEP enforcement against a willing party hoping to obtain a license under the FRANDterms could be equally applied, for the purpose of preventing possible harm through the use of standard technology, to AMA's regulation against the SEP enforcement[4]. We can observe from this Guideline's approach that JFTCadmitted incorporating the High Court's framework of the Abuse of Rightsprinciple under the Civil Code, as it is, to a legal framework of the anti-competitive IP enforcement regulation under the AMA.

In addition to the above, the IP Guideline also clarifies that the criteria for judgement of "a willing party hoping to obtain a license under the FRANDterms" shall consist of the following facts: a) whether the SEP holder indicates a prospective licensee any factual evidence of infringement, b) whether the SEP holder proposes its license terms with reasonable explanation, c) whether a prospective licensee timely responds to the SPE holder's proposal, and d) whether a prospective licensee sincerely negotiates in compliance with the commercial custom.

Overall, it is clear that the revision of IP Guideline is incorporating the previous legal framework of restriction on the SEP enforcement, which was prepared by the IP High Courtfor the judgement of the Abuse of Rightsprinciple under Article 1-3 in the Civil

---

3.*See* Takeuchi, IOT Business Model and Issues on IP Law, Competition Law and Information Law in Japan 79-82 (2018) [hereinafter *Takeuchi 2018*].
4.*JFTC IP Guideline* at Section 3-1-1-e & 4-2-4.

Code, into the judgement of the regulation under the AMA. However, further discussions on whether it was genuinely appropriate to apply these four criteria in the Abuse of Rightsprinciple's judgement under the Civil Code to the Private Monopolization's or Unfair Method of Transaction's judgement under the AMA would be expected in the academia.

1-3-3   One-Blue LLC Case (2016)

In the case of One-Blue LLC[5], a patent pool company of Blu-ray disc technology holding a number of SEP for the technology, the JFTCconcluded that One-Blue LLC's conduct of notifying an existence of its right of injunction claim against the prospective licensee, a manufacturer of Blu-ray disc products, based on its SEP for Blu-ray disc products to its retailers in the market shall be regarded as 'Interference with a Competitor's Transactions' in Article 14 of the General Designation and constitute a violation of the Unfair Trade Practicesregulation (Article 19, AMA) under the AMA.

Also, in a course of this decision, the JFTCexplicitly confirmed that the claim of injunction based on the SEP involving a declaration of FRANDlicense against a willing prospective licensee will constitute the violation of above-mentioned Section 4-2-(4) in the JFTC IP Guideline, as well as Abuse of Rightsin Article 1-3 of the Civil Code, and the claim of injunction based on the SEP, in this case, shall not be permissible[6].

1-4   Proposal of Compulsory License on SEP Enforcement (2017-2018)

1-4-1   Overview

Following the JFTC's revision of IP Guideline in 2016, in response to the progress of the AI/IoT business models and its related open IP transactions, the active roles of Non-Practicing Entities (hereinafter 'NPEs') received attention in the market of Japan around 2017[7]. Also, NPEs' collection and enforcement of patents[8]were presenting many discussions in relation to the IP policymaking in Japan[9].

5.Announcement of JFTC, Breach of Anti-monopoly Act by One-Blue LLC, 18 Nov. 2016 [hereinafter *One-Blue LLC Case*], *available at* https://www.jftc.go.jp/houdou/pressrelease/h28/nov/16111802.html.

6.Ishida, *Hyoujun hissutokkyo ni kakaru dokusenkinshihou jyou no mondai [Issues on Standard Essential Patents under Anti-monopoly Act]*, 72(1) Patent 86, 89-90 (2019), *available at* https://system.jpaa.or.jp/patent/viewPdf/3167.

7.The author hereby sincerely expresses its gratitude to Prof. Sir Robin Jacob from University College London, Prof. Ariel Ezrachi, Prof. Graeme Dinwoodie and Prof. Dev Gangjee from University of Oxford, Dr. Ariannna Andregianni from University of Edinburgh, and Dr Oleksandr Pastukhov from University of Malta, for their continued support to my research on discussions of the compulsory license approach in the EU and East Asian countries.

8.*See* Institute of Intellectual Property, Sangyou no hattatsu wo sogaisuru kanousei no aru kenrikoushi heno taiousaku ni kannsuru chousa kenkyuu houkokusho [Study report on countermeasures to enforcement of rights possibly restricting development of industry], Mar. 2009, *available at* https://dl.ndl.go.jp/view/download/digidepo_1248038_po_200200all.pdf?contentNo=1&alternativeNo=.

9.*See* Hienuki, *Nihon no biotechnology sangyou to kyousou seisaku [Japan biotechnology industry and competition policy]*, 9 Intellectual Property Law and Policy Journal 1, 15-16 (2006) [hereinafter *Hienuki 2006*], *available at* http://eprints.lib.hokudai.ac.jp/dspace/bitstream/2115/43461/1/9_1-21.pdf.

Under the situation, for the purpose of dealing with a possible conflict between NPEs and Japanese industry, the Japanese government took the initiative of the reform of Patents Act and started to study a new arbitration system on SEP disputes ('SEP Arbitration System'), which can be initiated by a sole petition from a prospective user of a patent, rather than a joint petition brought by the mutual agreement between a prospective user and the owner of the patent. Also, it was reported[10]that the employment of a new scheme of the license order, which will be given by the SEP Arbitration System's decision, was being discussed in the policy committee[11].

The intensive studies of this policy plan were scheduled during the year of 2017, and submission of the bill of Patents Act's reform was planned in 2018.However, this policy plan of unique SEP Arbitration System along with the new license order scheme was entirely suspended in the spring of 2018, due to concern about the possible disturbance of the global harmonization after the JPO Commissioner's opinion exchange with foreign governments at the end of 2017.

1-4-2 Analysis of Study and Suspension of SEP License Order Scheme

Under the Patents Act of Japan, the Japan Patent Office (hereinafter 'JPO') can order patents holders to grant a non-exclusive award license (hereinafter 'Award License') for some patents, on condition that the decision by the Commissioner of the JPO or the Minister of METI is made after confirming satisfaction of the statutory requirements[12]. This Award License is a kind of compulsory licenseto which the Agreement on Trade-Related Aspects of Intellectual Property Rights attached to the establishment of the World Trade Organization (hereinafter 'TRIPs Agreement') is providing a global framework and some limitations.

In the course of the JPO's studies on the SEP Arbitration System along with its new Award License plan, the legal interpretation of TRIPs Agreement by the WIPO's Standing Committee of Patents was carefully examined. More specifically, Article 30 and Article 31[13], along with Article 27, of TRIPs Agreement was closely focused on in the analysis.

Based on the legal interpretation in the report by the WIPO Standing Committee of

10.Industrial Structure Council, *The 20th Session of Patent Legislation Sub-Committee*, Apr. 2017, Attachment No.3-10 (Japan Patent Office, Study of new ADR system focusing on the Fourth Industrial Revolution) [hereinafter *Council Material 2017*], *available at* https://www.jpo.go.jp/resources/shingikai/sangyo-kouzou/shousai/tokkyo_shoi/document/20-shiryou/03.pdf.

11.*cf. Council Material 2017*.

12.*See* Article 83, 92 and 93, Patents Act of Japan.

13.Also, we should note that an academic discussion regarding 'ground approach' and 'process approach' exists on the effect of these articles.

Patents[14], JPO had finally reached its conclusion to stop the further study of the SEP Arbitration System and its new Award License plan and suspend the reform of Patents Act.

In the conclusion of the analysis by the JPO's working group, it was emphasized that the global common understanding of Article 31 of the TRIPs Agreement requires a necessity of "promotion of innovation under competitive surroundings" and necessity of "protection of patents system securing the public interests" for the judgement of "national emergency or other circumstances of extreme urgency" criteria of the compulsory licensesystem.

More precisely, in terms of the judgement of "national emergency or other circumstances of extreme urgency" criteria of the compulsory licensesystem. the WIPO's Standing Committee of Patents was mainly discussing only the situation of "securing national security or dealing with public health crises" and not expanding their scope of discussion to some specific field of technologies, such as the standard technology in the ICT industry. Based on this observation, we can observe that the Standing Committee, and its global common understanding, has not considered any SEP for the standard technology in the ICT industry as the objective of possible compulsory licenseorder under Article 31 of the TRIPs Agreement.

In addition, Article 27 of the TRIPs Agreement and its technology nondiscrimination principle should be carefully examined in relation with the discussion of the compulsory license order scheme solely applied to SEP for the standard technology in the ICT industryas well.

As a conclusion of those observations in the above, we can conclude that the SEP Arbitration System and its new Award License scheme cannot be regarded as the compulsory licensescheme for "securing national security or dealing with public health crises" and is not within the scope of discussion under Article 31 of the TRIPs Agreement based on the global common understanding shown in the Standing Committee's discussion. Also, the Award License scheme targeting solely at SEP for standard technology in the ICT industryis involving possible violation of Article 27 under the TRIPs Agreement and its technology nondiscrimination principle.

14.Standing Committee on the Law of Patents, WIPO, *Thirteenth Session, Geneva, March 23 to 27, 2009, Standards and Patents*, 18 Feb. 2009 [hereinafter *WIPO 2009A*], *available at* http://www.wipo.int/edocs/mdocs/scp/en/scp_13/scp_13_2.pdf. And, Standing Committee on the Law of Patents, WIPO, *Thirteenth Session, Geneva, March 23 to 27, 2009, Exclusions from Patentable Subject Matter and Exceptions and Limitation to the Rights*, 4 Feb. 2009 [hereinafter *WIPO 2009B*], *available at*https://www.wipo.int/edocs/mdocs/scp/en/scp_13/scp_13_3.pdf. Also *see* Standing Committee on the Law of Patents, WIPO, *Twenty-First Session, Geneva, November 3 to 7, 2014, Exceptions and Limitations to Patent Rights: Compulsory Licenses and/or Government Use* (Part I), 3 Nov. 2014. And, Standing Committee on the Law of Patents, WIPO, *Twenty-First Session, Geneva, November 3 to 7, 2014, Exceptions and Limitations to Patent Rights: Compulsory Licenses and/or Government Use* (Part II), 7 Nov. 2014.

However, in the author's opinion, it should be noted, in terms of this SEP Award License discussion, that there still can be a possible discussion of the compulsory licensescheme for "sanction to anti-competitive conducts" caused by the SEP enforcement. In this regard, we should remark for the further policy discussion in Japan that the foreign policy approach in Argentina, where the individual situations allowing "sanction to anti-competitive conducts" are explicitly provided in its legislation, provides some important preceding[15].

The author concludes that the policy plan of new compulsory licenseorder scheme for the 'sanction to anti-competitive conducts', as opposed to the SEP Award License scheme, would have been the option which JPO could choose in light of the harmonization with the global common understanding of Article 31 and Article 27 under the TRIPs Agreement's framework[16].

In conclusion, this policy plan of the SEP Arbitration System and new compulsory licenseorder system for SEP were entirely stopped in the spring of 2018 for the reason of the concern of disturbance of the global policy's harmonization under the TRIPs Agreement framework after the JPO Commissioner's opinion exchange with foreign governments at the end of 2017, and the reform of the Patents Act for this policy plan has been suspended until today.

1-5 SEP Negotiation Guideline by JPO (2018)

After the suspension of the policy plan of SEP Award License in the spring of 2018, the JPO was working on another guide for the SEP licensing, which analyzed possible employment of 'Comparable License Approach' and 'Top-down Approach'. As a result of the JPO's effort, the new 'Guide To Licensing Negotiations Involving Standard Essential Patents' (hereafter 'SEP Licensing Negotiations Guide') was announced in 2018[17].

The JPO's guidance provides the principles of licensing negotiations for SEP consisting of the following basic rules: (a) SEP licensing negotiations should be processed in accordance with the legal framework indicated by the IP High Courtin Apple vs. Samsung case (2014), and (b) 'Comparable License Approach' along with 'Top-down Approach', which was provided by the UK court's judgement in Unwired Planet vs.

15.*Takeuchi 2018* at 76-78.

16.In relation with discussions of the compulsory license scheme, Prof. Hienuki expressed his concern of emergence of industrial protectionism and disturbance of global harmonization under the TRIPs framework [*cf. Hienuki 2006* at 18].

17.Japan Patent Office, *Guide To Licensing Negotiations Involving Standard Essential Patents*, 5 Jun. 2018 [hereinafter *SEP Negotiations Guide*], *available at* https://www.jpo.go.jp/system/laws/rule/guideline/patent/document/seps-tebiki/guide-seps-en.pdf.

Huawei (2017)[18], should be employed in addition to the IP High Court framework for the precise calculation of the FRANDroyalty rate.

Also, the SEP Licensing Negotiations Guide emphasizes the importance of transparency and predictability in SEP licensing, in order to prevent future patent disputes and promote smooth licensing negotiations in the ICT industryand other fields, through the clarification of the lawful framework of SEP licensing practice based on the relevant court's judgments in Japan and foreign countries.

In summary, the author concludes that this JPO's guidance is the active government's policy work which tries to promote the formulation of the framework of FRAND licensing negotiations between the SEP holder and a prospective licensee and, through this formulation, reduce the unpredictability of the IP transaction in the FRAND licensing negotiations on SEP.

2   Situation in Europe

2-1   European Commission's Commitments on SEP Enforcement in Samsung Case (2014) and Motorola Mobility Case (2014)

In the Samsung Electronics and Motorola Mobility's SEP enforcement cases the European Commissionconfirmed its basic understanding on the restriction of SEP enforcement that, when a SEP implementer is willing to accept a license under the FRANDterms, a claim of injunctive relief based on the SEP shall be regarded as the abusive enforcement of the patent.

The European Commissionmade a decision of official commitment with Samsung Electronics in April 2014 that Samsung shall not file a lawsuit, for a period of 5 years, claiming an injunction based on its SEP for the mobile telecommunication technology against any party within European Economic Area (EEA) who agrees with the SEP license framework[19]. Samsung had filed multiple lawsuits against Apple Inc., claiming an injunctive relief at the German court and other EU member country's courts in this case.

Also, the European Commissiongave an order to Motorola Mobility, on the same day

---

18.Unwired Planet Int'l Ltd. v. Huawei Techs. Co. [2017] EWHC 711 (Pat) [hereinafter *Unwired Planet v. Huawei (2017)*].

19.European Commission, *Press release, Antitrust, Commission accepts legally binding commitments by Samsung Electronics on standard essential patent injunctions*, 29 Apr. 2014 [hereinafter *EC Samsung Case*], *available at* https://ec.europa.eu/commission/presscorner/detail/en/IP_14_490.

as the above-mentioned Samsung case, to stop the anti-competitive conduct on the grounds that Motorola Mobility's enforcement of SEP for the mobile telecommunication technology, which claimed injunction in the German court, shall constitute an abuse of market control power[20].

2-2. Huawei vs. ZTE Case (2015)

In this Court of Justice of the European Union (ECJ) case in 2015, ZTE Corporation argued the violation of EU Competition Law under Article 102 of the Treaty on the Functioning of the European Union (TFEU) regarding the SEP enforcement by Huawei Technologies Co. Ltd[21].

In response to the request from a German court, the Court of Justice made its judgement following the basic approach in the European Commission's commitments and clarified that the SEP holder should be obliged to grant a license to a prospective licensee who is willing to accept the license of SEP under the FRANDterms.

More precisely, under this framework of the restriction of SEP enforcement the court indicates that the SEP holder, who claims infringement of patent and its injunctive relief, must comply with the following conducts: a) the SEP holder makes a notification of patent infringement, which identifies the subject patent and the way of infringement, to an alleged infringer before bringing its legal action, b) if the alleged infringer expresses its willingness to agree a license agreement under the FRANDterms, and c) the SEP holder presents a specific and written offer of a license under the FRAND terms specifying the royalty rate along with the way of it is calculated. Also, if the alleged infringer does not accept that SEP holder the offer of a license under the FRAND terms, the alleged infringer must comply with the following actions: d) the alleged infringer promptly presents its own offer of a license under the FRAND terms, and e) if the SPE holder does not agree to the license offer, the alleged infringer provides appropriate security for its previous and future use of the SEP[22].

We can observe that the Court of Justice in this case had established the fundamental framework of judgement, the criteria of 'willingness to the FRANDlicense' and 'good

20. European Commission, *Press release, Antitrust, Commission finds that Motorola Mobility infringed EU competition rules by misusing standard essential patents*, 29 Apr. 2014 [hereinafter *EC Motorola Case*], *available at* https://ec.europa.eu/commission/presscorner/detail/en/IP_14_489.

21. Case C-170/13 *Huawei Technologies Co. Ltd v. ZTE Corp* ECLI:EU:C:2015:477; [2015] Bus. L.R. 1261, [2016] R.P.C. 4, CJEU. [hereinafter *Huawei v. ZTE Case*]. Also *see* Killick, ECJ rips up Orange Book! New standards in Europe for SEP injunctions, http://competitionlawblog.kluwercompetitionlaw.com/2015/09/04/ecj-rips-up-orange-book-new-standards-in-europe-for-sep-injunctions/, last visited 1 Aug. 2020.

22. *Id.* at para 77.

faith conducts in the negotiations' (the so-called 'Huawei Rules'), in the EU countries about situations the injunctive relief based on SEP can be allowed by the court.

2-3   Communication from European Commission of 'Setting out the EU approach to Standard Essential Patents' (2017)

Following the commitments in the Samsung and Motorola Mobility cases and the ECJ judgement, in November 2017 the European Commissionprepared the communication of its new guidance on the restriction of SEP enforcement, based on its analysis in those cases, along with the policy report of the IP enforcement for promoting innovation and investment in the EU market[23].

In the new guidance, the European Commissioninsisted on the importance of a fair and balanced system for SEP enforcement. The commission's guidance declares that, through such a fair and balanced system, a SEP implementer will be able to access standardized technology under transparent and predictable procedures, and the SEP holder can maintain an appropriate incentive to future R&D investment and return from those investments.

More specifically, the guidance points out the four elements required for the fair and balanced system on the SEP enforcement as follows: (a) transparency on SEP, (b) principle of SEP licensing, (c) predictability on SEP enforcement, and (d) open-source software and SEP[24].

Firstly, the guidance emphasizes the necessity of securing '(a) transparency on SEP' in its 'Chapter 1. INCREASING TRANSPARENCY ON SEPS EXPOSURE' . In this chapter, the European Commissionrequires standard developing organizations to improve the quality of the patents declaration database and offers its cooperation for promoting a process of quality improvement.

Secondly, the guidance introduces the importance of '(b) principle of SEP licensing' based on the FRANDterms in its 'Chapter 2. GENERAL PRINCIPLES FOR FRAND LICENSING TERMS FOR SEPS' . The European Commissionclarifies the licensing principle based on the FRAND terms that the FRAND royalty should be calculated on

---

23.European Commission, *Communication from the Commission to the European Parliament, the Council and the European Economic and Social Committee :Setting out the EU approach to Standard Essential Patents*, 29 Nov. 2017, *available at* https://ec.europa.eu/docsroom/documents/26583.

24.*See Id.* at Section 1.1, 2.1, 3.1 & 4.

the basis of the economic value of patented technology as opposed to the economic value of a product incorporating the patented technology.

Following the above, the European Commission made a comment on 'c) predictability on SEP enforcement' in its 'Chapter 3. A PREDICTABLE ENFORCEMENT ENVIRONMENT FOR SEPS'. This chapter provides the principle of negotiations that both the SEP owner and a SEP implementer should negotiate on a FRANDlicensing of SEP in good faith, and an injunctive relief based on SEP shall be granted to the SEP owner solely against a SEP implementer in bad faith, subject to the proportionality assessment, who is not willing to obtain a SEP license under the FRAND terms.

Finally, the European Commissionalso discusses '(d) open-source software and SEP' in its 'Chapter 4. OPEN SOURCE AND STANDARDS'. In order to maintain a good relationship between the open-source community and standard developing organizations, the importance of collaborative work on the framework of SEP enforcement among the interested parties is emphasized, and the European Commission's active support for the analysis work in this matter is offered in the guidance.

2-4 Commission Decision of 'Setting up a group of experts on licensing and valuation of standard essential patents (2018)'

In addition to the communication of 'Setting out the EU approach to Standard Essential Patents' (2017), the European Commission announced that it would set up an experts group for analyzing the licensing and valuation of SEP in July 2018[25]. The establishment of the experts group was launched, in response to the European Commission's proposal in the communication, for a purpose of gathering further knowledge from the industry about the practice of SEP licensing, index of patents valuation and decisive factors of the FRANDterms.

According to this European Commission's decision, it is expected that the expert group will conduct multiple actions on the licensing and valuation of SEP as follows: '(a) to facilitate an exchange of experience and good practice in the field of licensing and valuation of Standard Essential Patents (SEPs)', '(b) to provide the Commission with the necessary economic, legal and technical expertise regarding evolving industry practices related to the licensing of SEPs, the sound valuation of intellectual property, and the

---

25.European Commission, *Commission decision, Setting up a group of experts on licensing and valuation of standard essential*, 5 Jul. 2018,*available at* patents https://ec.europa.eu/transparency/regexpert/index.cfm?do=groupDetail.groupDetailDoc&id=37653&no=1.

determination of FRANDlicensing terms', '(c) to assist the Commission in the monitoring of SEP licensing markets to inform any policy measures that may be required for ensuring a balanced framework for smooth, efficient and effective licensing of SEPs', and '(d) to assist the Commission in obtaining information on licensing and valuation practices in accordance with the Communication from the Commission on Setting out the EU approach to Standard Essential Patents'[26].

The appointment period of those members in the experts group is planned to be 2 years. Those members may be reappointed after the 2 years, and the appointment period can be extended.

2-5　Unwired Planet vs. Huawei (2017, 2018) and Other Recent Cases

In parallel with the European Commission's efforts on the framework of SEP enforcement in the above, the England and Wales High Court (EWHC) provided its judgement, which was generally following the basic unders;tanding showed in the above-mentioned European Commission's commitments (2014) with Samsung Electronics and Motorola Mobile on their mobile telecommunication technology, on SEP enforcement in the Unwired Planet vs. Huawei case (2017)[27].

In this UK case, the 'Comparable License Approach', along with the supplemental 'Top-Down Approach', was employed as the primary tool for calculating the reasonable royalty under the FRANDterms for SEP licensing[28].

Firstly, the UK court introduced the framework of 'Comparable License Approach' in which the calculation of the reasonable royalty under the FRAND terms should be based on the royalty rates in comparable license agreements previously agreed by the SEP holder.

The court started its analysis on the previous license agreements executed by Ericsson corporation, the prior patents holder who assigned the subject patents portfolio to Unwired Planet, in this case. After obtaining the information of those agreements, the license terms of every agreement were 'unpacked' into each patent basis, and its analysis work for calculating the FRANDroyalty in the 'One-way' unilateral license between Ericsson and each licensee was conducted. Through the confirmation of comparable agreements and analysis work of the license terms, the UK court 'virtually'

26.*Id.* at Article 2.

27.*Unwired Planet v. Huawei (2017).*

28.It should be noted that some European scholarly opinions insist that Huawei v. ZTE case (2015), as well as Unwired Planet v. Huawei case (2017), should have maintained the 'exceptional circumstances' test, which has been employed in the refusal of license cases, as apposed to newly employing the 'willing prospective licensee' test. *See Goikoetxea 2019* at 69-72.

concluded the estimated royalty rate of the SEP in the Ericsson's 'One-way' unilateral license.

More precisely, the court calculated the estimated unilateral license's royalty rate as 0.0062%, which was calculated by Ericsson's unilateral license's royalty rate of 0.80% and the relative ratio as 7.69% between LTE mobile telecommunication technology patent portfolio and Ericsson's entire patent portfolio. Based on those numbers the Unwired Planet's estimated entire cumulative royalty rate for the LTE patent portfolio was finally concluded as 8.8%. This royalty rate is in accordance with the request from major companies in the ICT industry, such as Ericsson, Nokia, NTT Docomo, NEC and Sony[29], that entire cumulative royalty rate should be less than 10% in every case.

Based on the observation in the above, the author concludes that the England and Wales High Court in the Unwired Planet vs Huawei case reaches a proper conclusion by appropriately using the 'Comparable License Approach' along with the supplemental 'Top-down Approach' .

Following the High Court judgement, in response to the appeal in this case the Court of Appeal provided its judgement in October 2018[30]. However the appeal was dismissed by the Court of Appeal's judgement, and the judgement still maintains the previous legal framework in the above, which provided in the High Court's judgement, with no material change.

However, it should be noted that some European scholarly opinions insist that Huawei v. ZTE case (2015), as well as Unwired Planet v. Huawei case (2017), should have maintained the 'exceptional circumstances' test, which has been employed in the refusal of license cases, as apposed to newly employing the 'willing prospective licensee' test[31]. The author expects that the court may add some extra criteria derived from the

---

29.Deng et al., *Comparative Analysis of Court-Determined FRAND Royalty Rates*, 32 Antitrust 46, 50 (2018), *available at* https://www.americanbar.org/content/dam/aba/administrative/antitrust_law/Summer18-LeonardC.pdf.

30.Unwired Planet Int'l Ltd. v. Huawei Techs. Co., [2018] EWCA (Civ) 2344 [hereinafter *Unwired Planet v. Huawei Case (2018)*]. In response to Huawei's appeal, the Supreme Court of UK made the judgement in this case on 26 August, 2020 (UKSC 37 [2020], *available at* https://www.supremecourt.uk/cases/docs/uksc-2018-0214-judgment.pdf.). In this judgement the Supreme Court maintained the framework provided by the Court of Appeal and clearly pointed out that a hard-edged approach on patent holder's obligation of 'non-discriminatory' licence is excessively strict. *See* Mutimear & Vary, UK Supreme Court rules on FRAND approach in Unwired Planet and Conversant, Aug.2020, https://search.yahoo.co.jp/search?ei=UTF-8&fr=mcafeess1&p=commensurate.

31.*Goikoetxea 2019* at 69-72 , Cascón, *La problemática de las patentes indispensables en estándares técnicos y la eficacia de los compromisos de licencia en términos FRAND* [*The problem of technical standards essential patents and the effectiveness of FRAND license commitments*], 3 REVISTA ELECTRÓNLOA DE DIREITO 1,46-49 (2016) [hereinafter *Cascón 2016*], and Petit, *Injunctions for Frand-Pledged SEPs: The Quest for an Appropriate Test of Abuse Under Article 102 TFEU*, 9(3) EUROPEAN COMPETITION JOURNAL 677, 686 & 719 (2013) [hereinafter *Petit 2013*]. Also, *cf.* Goikoetxea, *Why* 'exceptional circumstances' test to the 'willing prospective licensee' test in any future marginal case[32] of SEP enforcement where disturbance of market competition caused by the refusal of SEP license is not very clear.

Also, in the German case, Sisvel vs. Haier in March 2017[33], although the Higher Regional Court of Düsseldorf applied the restrictive criterion of 'non-discriminatory' in the FRANDterms to the offer of license from the SEP holder[34], the German court maintained the fundamental framework of the Huawei Rules established by the ECJ in 2015[35].

Following the Higher Regional Court judgement in the above, in May 2020 the German Federal Supreme Court has made a decision statement regarding recovering the strict requirement of 'willingness' to the prospective licensee's conducts[36]. The author observes that, through the Supreme Court's decision, the German court would recover the balanced criteria of the FRAND terms and maintain the proper framework of the Huawei Rules[37].

---

the Magill criteria should have been reviewed in IMS Health and the effectiveness of compulsory licence, 40 (1) European Competition Law Review 24 (2019), Peralta, Una vuelta a la aplicacion de la doctrina de las facilidades esenciales (essential facilities) a la propiedad intelectual e industrial [A return to the application of the doctrine of essential facilities (essential facilities) to intellectual and industrial property], 19 REVISTA DE DERECHO DE LA COMPETENCIA Y LA DISTRIBUOIÓN 14 (2016), and Petit, EU Competition Law Analysis of FRAND Disputes,inTHE CAMBRIDGE HANDBOOK TECHNOLOGICAL STANDARDIZATION LAW: COMPETIION, ANTITRUST, AND PATENTS 29 (Contreras ed., 2017). Having those opinions, the author believes with regard to Japan's practice that JFTC should employ an additional criteria of 'complete elimination of the competition in the downstream market' to its 'willing prospective licensee' test for enforcement of FRAND declared SEPs in Section 4-2-(4) [Unfair Trade Practices] of JFTC IP Guideline.

32.Cf. Sarah Morgan, Germany's Cartel Office weighs in on Nokia/Daimler SEP dispute, 24 June, 2020, http:/ /www.klaka.com/fileadmin/Presseberichte/2020/Kurtz_World_IP_Review_Nokia_Daimler_SEP_dispute.pdf, last visited 1 Aug. 2020.

33.OLG Düsseldorf, 30 March 2017, File No. I-15 U 66/15, OLG Düsseldorf, 30 March 2017, File No. I-15 U 66/15.

34.Id. at para 251.

35.Id. at para 240.

36.Hearing before the Federal Court of Justice on 5 May 2020 and decision – KZR 36/17.

37.See Juve Nachrichten, First German BGH ruling on FRAND rules since 2015: Sisvel v. Haier, 26 Jun. 2020, https:// legal-patent.com/licenses/first-german-bgh-ruling-on-frand-rules-since-2015-sisvel-v-haier, last visited 1 Apr. 2020.

Chapter 5

SEP enforcement : Implication of Samsung's SEP Cases for East Asia

1   Overview

In response to the decisions in Samsung's standard essential patent (hereinafter 'SEP') enforcement cases in Japan and Europe introduced in the previous chapters, new policy-making on the enforcement of IP incorporated in standard technologies has been discussed in Japan. Also, it should be noted that the policy-making discussions in Korea and China have been greatly accelerated, especially in the field of the ICT industry, by the decisions in Samsung's SEP enforcement cases.

In this regard, as analyzed in the previous chapter, we should firstly focus on the decision in the European Commission(hereinafter 'EC')[1]on Samsung's SEP enforcement of claiming an injunction against Apple's use of the standard technology and the following judgement by the European Court of Justice(hereinafter 'ECJ') in the Huawei vs. ZTE case[2]. Having these European decisions, we can observe in East Asian countries, i.e., Japan, Korea and China, that their policy-making and court judgement are generally following the legal framework of the restriction of SEP enforcement indicated by those European decisions.

Firstly, as we confirmed in the previous chapter, in Japan the IP High Courtprovided its judgement on the enforcement of SEP, as introduced in the previous chapter, in the Apple vs. Samsung case (2014) and, following this judgement, the Japan Fair Trade Commission (hereinafter 'JFTC') had published its revised guideline, the Guideline for Use of Intellectual Property under the Anti-Monopoly Act (hereinafter 'IP Guideline'), which newly introduces a regulation on the enforcement of IP incorporated in standard technology under the Anti-Monopoly Act (hereinafter 'AMA').
In addition to this, it should be remarked that after the IP High Court's judgement and the JFTC's revision of the guideline, the Japan Patent Office (hereinafter 'JPO') has reviewed the reform plan of the Japanese Patent Act (hereinafter "JPA") and announced the new guidance for negotiations of the SEP license and its royalty under the fair, reasonable, and non-discriminatory (hereinafter 'FRAND') terms.

In Korea, following the aforementioned situation in Japan, in response to the decisions in Samsung's SEP enforcement, the Korea Fair Trade Commission (hereinafter 'KFTC') had announced its IP guideline which clarifies the restriction on enforcement of the IP incorporated in standard technology under the Monopoly Regulations and Fair Trade Act. However, some industry associations were concerned about the ambiguity of its

---

1.EC Samsung Case.

2.Huawei v. ZTE Case.

regulation policy. It was concerned that this guideline could jeopardize the progress of technological innovation and R&D incentives in the Korean market.

Also in China, knowing the decisions of Samsung's SEP enforcement cases, the Chinese government is actively providing new guidelines through several Chinese government organizations.

In the course of the Chinese government's effort, the State Administration for Industry and Commerce (hereinafter 'SAIC') and the National Development and Reform Commission (hereinafter 'NDRC') have prepared their guidelines on abusive enforcement of the IP incorporated in standard technology.

As well as the Korean guideline, it is worried that those guidelines could prevent, due to the aggressive intervention in IP enforcement, progress of technological innovation and R&D incentives in the market of China.

This chapter will introduce examples of the regulation policy on enforcement of IP incorporated in standard technology in the aforementioned East Asian countries and discuss the possible emergence of 'Regulatory Competition' circumstances[3].

Also, this chapter will consider the possible excessive intervention in the enforcement of IP incorporated in the de-facto standard technology, rather than the de-jure standard technology, by authorities in East Asian countries. The author will step into an analysis of the European Essential Facilitiesdoctrine and its possible unique interpretation by the authorities.

2 Regulation Policy on Enforcement of IP Related to Standard Technology in Korea and China

2-1 Situation of Korea

2-1-1 Overview: KFTC IP Guideline (2000, Revised 2009, 2014, 2016)

The Korea Fair Trade Commission (hereinafter 'KFTC') announced a revision of its guideline of IP rights enforcement, the Review Guidelines on Unfair Exercise of Intellectual Property Rights (hereinafter 'KFTCIP Guideline'), at the end of 2014[4]. It is reported that the KFTC had an intention to restrict the abusive enforcement of IP

3.Emergence of the 'Regulatory Competition' situation was firstly discussed among the study group members in the IPR Policy Conference (1 Jun. 2017, Sofia, Bulgaria) of the MAPPING Project [https://observatory.mappingtheinternet.eu/page/ipr].

4.Korea Fair Trade Commission, *Review Guidelines on Unfair Exercise of Intellectual Property Rights*, 12 Aug. 2009, Revised 17 Dec. 2014 [hereinafter *KFTC Guideline 2014*], *available at* http://www.ftc.go.kr/www/cmm/fms/FileDown.do?atchFileId=FILE_000000000079690&fileSn=0.

rights by any giant global company through this revision of the guideline[5].

On the other hand, it was of concern to the industry that this revision could provide excessive restrictions on the enforcement of IP rights and cause a possible disincentive to technological development in the R&D market[6].

In this regard, we should pay attention to a statement in the KFTCIP Guideline about its restriction policy on enforcement of the IP rights incorporated in de-facto standard technology[7].

The guideline provided an unclear definition of 'standard technology' which could cover both de-jure standard technology and de-facto standard technology.

The author observes on the unclear definition that the KFTC might have not correctly differentiated de-facto standard technology from de-jure standard technology in the context of its restriction policy on enforcement of the IP rights incorporated in standard technology. This confusion of de-jure standard technology and de-facto standard technology in that context could be caused by the KFTCs' misunderstanding of the preceding case decisions by courts or authorities.

In response to the critics of the above, in 2016 the KFTCannounced its further revision to delete the statement of de-facto standard technology and limit the definition of 'standard technology' to exclude de-facto standard technologies from the objective of the KFTC IP Guideline in this context[8].

2-1-2 Analysis of the KFTC IP Guideline

The KFTC IP Guideline's Section III-3-B indicates that a patent owner can, to a reasonable extent, refuse to grant a license in order to protect its rights, and the refusal

---

5. Institute of Intellectual Property, *Kokusai Chizai Seido Houkokusho (Heisei 27th)* [*Study Report of International IP Legislation 2015*], Mar.2016, 65-66 [hereinafter *International IP Report H27*], *available at* https://warp.da.ndl.go.jp/info:ndljp/pid/10322385/www.jpo.go.jp/shiryou/toushin/chousa/pdf/tripschousahoukoku/27_all.pdf.

6. *Id.* at 79-81.

7. *KFTC Guideline 2014* at Section II-5-A. *See* the statement of Note in II-5-A-4: 'This applies not only to standard technologies set by standards organizations, but also to technologies widely used as de-facto standard technologies in related areas, such as technology selected as must-use technology when bidding for public organization projects'. This statement of Note was later entirely deleted by the revised KFTC Guideline on 23 March 2016, *available at* http://www.ftc.go.kr/eng/cop/bbs/selectBoardList.do?key=2855&bbsId=BBSMSTR_000000003632&bbsTyCode=BBST11. Also *see International IP Report H27* at 79-81.

8. Korea Fair Trade Commission, *KFTC initiates public comment period on the amendment to its IP guidelines — The proposed guidelines amend the definition of SEPs and address matters relating to de facto SEPs —*, 2, 16 Dec.2015 [hereinafter *KFTC Guideline Amendment 2016*].

of license is, in principle, a fair exercise of patent[9].

Notwithstanding the above, the guideline points out that some conducts can constitute unfair refusal of license. It asserts that the following conducts should be deemed as equivalent to refusal of license: a) making other parties refuse to grant a license, b) requesting an excessive royalty payment which is practically or economically impossible to make, and c) other conducts causing the equivalent result as a refusal of license.

More precisely, the KFTCIP Guideline insists that the following arbitrary conducts are likely to restrict a fair trade and to be regarded as a conduct beyond the extent of a fair exercise of patent: a) collaborating with competing enterprises to refuse to grant a license to a particular enterprise without justifiable reasons, b) unfairly refusing to grant a license to a particular enterprise, and c) refusing to grant a license for an unjust purpose such as making another enterprise accept the patent owner's unfair license terms[10].

Especially, in terms with the conduct of 'b) unfairly refusing to grant a license to particular enterprise' and the technical standard, the guideline provided, in 2014, an additional explanation in its footnote as follows: *'The act of refusing to grant a license is likely to be determined as unfair especially when the purpose of such refusal is related to restricting competition in the relevant market; when the technology, for which the license was refused, is an essential element in business activities; when it is difficult to secure alternative supply channel for the patented technology; when the technology, like a technical standard, has a great influence on the relevant market; and when the refusal by the patentee to grant a license, despite the patentee not having any intention to work the technology, excessively impedes the use of the technology'* [11].

It should be remarked that the footnote of the guideline explicitly mentions a refusal of license for the patented technology as 'an essential element in business activities' in the market. However the definition of 'essential element' is unclear, and it can be easily expanded to an approach of the expanded European 'Exceptional Circumstances' test or the European Essential Facilitiesdoctrine.

This unclear criteria for judgement of the abusive refusal of patents license could cause a possible negative effect on the incentive to develop technology in the R&D market. Some global companies were sharply pointing out this concern in their opinions[12].

9.Korea Fair Trade Commission, *Review Guidelines on Unfair Exercise of Intellectual Property Rights*, 12 Aug. 2009, Revised 23 Mar. 2016 [hereinafter *KFTC Guideline 2016*], *available at* http://www.ftc.go.kr/eng/cop/bbs/selectBoardList.do?key=2855&bbsId=BBSMSTR_000000003632&bbsTyCode=BBST11

10.*KFTC Guideline 2016* at Section III-3-B-1, 2 & 3.

11.*KFTC Guideline 2014* at Section III-3-B-2.

12.*International IP Report H27* at 79-81.

In response to concern from the industry, the KFTCentirely deleted the description of 'an essential element in business activities' through the revision of the KFTC IP Guideline in 2016. Instead of the description of 'an essential element in business activities', the revision in 2016 employs the alternative description of 'impractical to produce, supply, or sell any product or service without using the technology for which licensing is refused, leading to inaccessibility to relevant markets' and provides more clarification of its criteria of restriction of refusal of license by requiring the condition of 'inaccessibility to relevant markets' [13]. This prompt revision by the KFTCshould be positively accepted by the industry and academia.

In addition to the above, the KFTC IP Guideline's Section III-5-A remarks that a conduct of manipulating a standardization process through not disclosing its patent during the process, for the purpose of forcing its unfair licensing terms on other enterprises, could constitute an unfair trade of conduct in the market, and this non-disclosure conduct should be regarded as an act beyond the extent of a lawful exercise of patent.

In this regard, the KFTCIP Guideline designates the following as possible unfair conducts: a) *'In the process of discussion for the designation of standard technologies, acts of unfairly agreeing to conditions limiting the price, volume, regions, counterparts and technology improvement of the trade'* , b) *'Acts of unfairly not disclosing information of patents applied for or registered in order to increase the possibility of being designated as a standard technology or to avoid prior consultations on the conditions of granting of licenses'* , c) *'Acts of avoiding or circumventing licensing on FRANDterms to strengthen market dominance or to exclude competitors'* , d) *'Acts of unfairly rejecting the licensing of a standard essential patent'* , e) *'Acts of unfairly imposing discriminatory conditions when licensing standard essential patents or of imposing an unreasonable level of royalty'* , and f) *'An act of imposing conditions unfairly restricting the exercise of patent rights held by licensees or act of unfairly imposing conditions of cross licensing of non-standard essential patents held by licensees'* [14].

In relation with the designated conduct of e) *'Acts of unfairly imposing discriminatory*

13.*KFTC Guideline 2016* at Section III-3-B-2. The revised footnote of Section III-3-B-2 provides as follows: *'[Note] When determining whether licensing is refused unfairly,the following factors can be considered: whether the intent or purpose of refusing the license is related to restricting competition in the relevant market; whether it is impractical to produce, supply, or sell any product or service without using the technology for which licensing is refused, leading to inaccessibility to relevant markets or inevitable and continuous less-competitive position in relevant markets; whether a particular enterpriser monopolizes and controls the relevant technology; whether it is legally or economically impractical to obtain alternative technology to the technology for which licensing is refused; or whether refusing the license has restricted competition or is likely to restrict competition'* .

14.*KFTC Guideline 2016* at Section III-5-A-1, 2, 3, 4, 5 & 6.

conditions when licensing standard essential patents or of imposing an unreasonable level of royalty' , a unique statement on de-facto standard technology was made by the KFTCin its footnote as follows: *'This applies not only to standard technologies set by standards organizations, but also to technologies widely used as de-facto standard technologies in related areas, such as technology selected as must-use technology when bidding for public organization projects'* [15].

As stated in the above, we can observe that the KFTC confuses de-jure standard technology and de-facto standard technology in the context of its judgement of the abusive enforcement of IP rights. The author believes that the KFTC's confusion of de-jure standard technology and de-facto standard technology could be caused by the KFTC's misunderstanding of the preceding decisions by courts and authorities.

In response to criticism of this apparent confusion, the KFTCfinally announced a further revision of the guideline by deleting this footnote statement on de-facto standard technology in March 2016 and limiting the definition of 'standard technology' as an objective under this guideline in this context[16]. Also, in accordance with this revision, the KFTCentirely deleted the language of de-facto standard (*'technologies actually used widely as the standard in the relevant technology area'*)from the definition of 'Standard Technologies' in Section 3. Definitions of Part I. General Provision in the guideline and clarified that the IP rights incorporated in a de-facto standard will be excluded from the scope of the guideline.

The KFTC's prompt revisions which exclude de-facto standard technologies from the scope of the guideline should be positively accepted by the industry[17].

2-1-3 KFTC Decision in Qualcomm Case (2017)

In the Qualcomm case[18], the KFTCaccused Qualcomm, Inc. of rejection of license on SEP for wireless communication technology against the Samsung company in 2017.

In this case Qualcomm ran two streams of business: (a) a patent licensing business conducted by Qualcomm Incorporated and (b) a modem chipset business conducted by Qualcomm Technologies and CDMA Technologies Asia-Pacific PTE Limited.

In the situation in the above, it was discussed that Qualcomm could abusively use its

---

15.*KFTC Guideline 2014* at Section III-5-A-4.

16.*KFTC Guideline Amendment 2016* at 2.

17.In contrast, it should be noted on the situation of Japan that JFTC has not taken an action, until today, of revising a language covering the both de-jure standard and de-facto standard in Section 2-4-2 of JFTC IP Guideline.

18.Decision of KFTC, No. 2017-025, 2015Sigam2118 (S. Kor.), *available at* https://link.springer.com/chapter/10.1007/978-981-13-1232-8_9.

SEP licensing business negotiations to promote its another business, the modem chipset business, to mobile phone manufacturers. The KFTCaccused Qualcomm of using the SEP negotiations on wireless communication technology, under its 'no-license, no-chip' licensing policy, as 'leverage' for unjustly spreading its market share of the modem chipset business.

Although Qualcomm requested a consent decree from the KFTC in November 2016, it was denied by the KFTC. After the dismissal of Qualcomm's consent decree motion, the KFTC decided to fine Qualcomm 1.03 trillion won (approximately 850 million USD), along with applying corrective measures in December 2016.

The author observes that, after the announcement of the revisions of KFTC's IP Guideline in 2014 and 2016, the KFTCcarefully followed the legal framework on SEP enforcement prepared by the guideline and applied it to this case.   More concretely, we can observe that the KFTC regarded Qualcomm's rejection of license as a 'leverage' tool for expansion of its market controlling power in the technology marketto the relevant market, and Qualcomm's 'no-chip and no-license' policy to mobile phone manufacturers was considered abusive licensing policy in accordance with the framework of the KFTCIP Guideline.

2-1-4   Korean Patents Act reform for the punitive damage system (2019)

In Korea, the reform bill of the Korean Patents Act which incorporates the punitive damages system passed through the parliament in December 2018 and became effective in June 2019[19].

This Korean punitive damages system sets the amount of damages to be paid by the willful infringer of patents infringement to be three times higher than an amount of actual damages. Under this new system, the court will make a judgement on the willful infringement by assessing the following factors provided in Article 128-9 of the Patents Act: a) superior position of infringer, b) willfulness or recognition of damages risk, c) amount of damages caused by infringement, d) infringer's economic benefit obtained from infringement, e) period and times of infringement, f) amount of the fine against infringement, and g) infringer's effort of avoiding damages[20].

The academia in Korea positively accepts this reform of the punitive damages system

---

19.NGB Corporation, Kankoku choubatsuteki songaibaishou dounyuu he [Revision of Korean Patents Act incorporating the punitive damages system], 18 Jan. 2019, https://www.ngb.co.jp/ip_articles/detail/1652.html, last visited on 1 May. 2020.

20.*See* Article 128-8 & 9 of Patents Act of Korea, *available* *at* http://www.choipat.com/menu31.php?id=14&category=0&keyword=.

as this system will make SEP prospective licensees start their faithful license negotiation in accordance with the KFTCIP Guideline which restricts the injunctive relief based on the abusive enforcement of SEP[21]. However, the author observes that this punitive damages system is an excessive reaction to the restriction of SEP enforcement under the KFTC IP Guideline. We should remember that the KFTC IP Guideline carefully excluded de-jure standard technology, and its related IP rights enforcement, from the scope of restriction under the guideline in the revision of 2016 and thus recovered the proper balance between exclusivity held by the SEP owner for de-jure standard and exploitation promoted by its prospective licensees.

It is the author's opinion that we should be most cautious about employment of the punitive damages system in the Patents Law framework under the Civil Law systems, since the punitive damages system can be abused by Non-Practicing Entities (NPE) under the Civil Law's automatic injunctive relief system[22]. Also, we can observe that this kind of excessive regulation in the IP law policy could be a result of the 'regulatory competition' [23]and may bring further 'regulatory competition' situations among countries in the East Asia region.

2-2   Situation of China

2-2-1   Overview

The Chinese government executed the Chinese Anti-Monopoly Act (hereinafter 'CAMA') in August 2007. Article 55 of the CAMA states that abusive exercise of IP rights which excludes or restricts market competition can constitute a violation of CAMA[24].

CAMA

Article 55

This Law does not govern the conduct of business operators to exercise their intellectual property rights under laws and relevant administrative regulations on intellectual property rights; however, business operators' conduct to eliminate or restrict market competition by

---

21.Institute of Intellectual Property, *Hyoujun hissu tokkyo wo meguru funsou no kaiketsu jittai ni kansuru chousa kenkyuu hokokusho* [*Research report of dispute resolution of standard essential patents*], 106-107, Mar. 2019 [hereinafter *IIP SEP Report H30*], *available at* https://www.jpo.go.jp/resources/report/sonota/document/zaisanken-seidomondai/2018_10_zentai.pdf

22.*See*Institute of Intellectual Property, *Kenrikoushi taiyou no tayouka wo fumaeta tokkyoken no arikata ni kannsuru chousa kenkkyuu houkokusho* [*Research Report of patent legislation in response to diversity of patents enforcement*], 119-121, Feb. 2011 [hereinafter *IIP Enforcement Report H22*], *available at* https://www.globalipdb.inpit.go.jp/jpowp/wp-content/uploads/2014/05/fa56b71cf7f9a09ce3994c0ab8a47dbb.pdf.

23.The 'Regulatory Competition' situation was introduced at first in the IPR Policy Conference (1 Jun. 2017, Sofia, Bulgaria) of the MAPPING Project [https://observatory.mappingtheinternet.eu/page/ipr].

24.Anti-Monopoly Act of China, *available at* http://www.fdi.gov.cn/1800000121_39_1899_0_7.html.

abusing their intellectual property rights shall be governed by this Law.

In addition to Article 55 of CAMA above, the State Administration for Industry and Commerce of the People's Republic of China (hereinafter 'SAIC') announced its new guideline on the conduct of excluding and restricting the competition through abuse of IP rights (hereinafter 'SAIC IP Guideline') in April 2015 and made this guideline effective in August of the same year. This announcement was an important first step for the Chinese government's policy on the restriction of IP rights enforcement[25].

The SAICIP Guideline provides a basic understanding of abusive enforcement of IP rights incorporated in standard technology under the CAMA. However, it should be noted in the guideline that SAIC's authority on the CAMA is limited to non-pricing anti-competitive conduct only[26].

Also, we should remark that the SAIC IP Guideline does not clearly differentiate de-facto standard technology from de-jure standard technology in the context of abusive IP enforcement related to standard technology[27]. The industry is concerned that this broad definition of standard technology in the guideline can lead to a reduction in its incentive to develop technology in the R&D market[28].

In addition, the software industry of the United States clearly points out that the market controlling power cannot be easily obtained by owners of software IP rights. In most cases, widely spread software technology can be easily replaced by alternative software technology because of the technological uniqueness of software language and programming[29]. The software industry is requesting a different treatment of restriction on software IP rights under the guideline.

---

25. State Administration for Industry and Commerce of the People's Republic of China, *Guideline on the Conduct of Excluding and Restricting the Competition through Abuse of IP Rights*, 7 Apr. 2015 [hereinafter *SAIC Guideline*],*available at* https://www.jetro.go.jp/ext_images/world/asia/cn/ip/law/pdf/origin/admin20150801.pdf, *and* https://www.unifab.com/wp-content/uploads/2016/06/Nouveau-Rglement-de_SAIC.pdf. Also *see* State Administration for Industry and Commerce of the People's Republic of China, *Request for public comments on SAIC Guideline draft*, 11 Jun.2014, *available at* https://www.amt-law.com/asset/pdf/bulletins7_pdf/140624_02.pdf.

26. *International IP Report H27* at 82-84.

27. *Id.* at 83.

28. *Cf.* Article 7 of SAIC Guideline provides as follows: '*Without justifiable reason,an enterprise maintaining a dominant position in the market may not refuse to grant a license to the other enterprises to use it's IPR with reasonable license conditions, if it's IP constitutes an essential facility for manufacturing or business activities in the market. And, it provides in terms of judgement of an essential facility that in order to make a judgement about whether IPR constitutes an essential facility the following conditions must be considered such as a) there exists no reasonable alternative to the IP in a relevant market for the other enterprises, b) the refusal of granting a license of IPR will cause adversely effect to competition and innovation in a relevant market, and c) the grant of IP license will not cause unreasonable damage to the enterprise*'.

29. *International IP Report H27* at 84.

In addition to the SAIC's guideline in the above, the National Development and Reform Commission (hereinafter 'NDRC') published its own CAMA guideline on abusive enforcement of IP rights and requested public opinions in December 2015. At the same time, the SAICannounced another guideline of CAMA enforcement on the exercise of IP rights along with a request for public opinions in February 2016[30].

2-2-2 Analysis of the SAIC IP Guideline (2015)

Article 7 of the SAICIP Guideline states that, without justifiable reason, an enterprise maintaining its dominant position in a market may not refuse to grant a license with reasonable license terms to other enterprises, in the event the subject IP constitutes an essential facility for manufacturing or other business activities in the market. The guideline provides that judgement of the essential facility should be made by the following criteria: a) whether or not there exists a reasonable alternative to the IP rights in the relevant market, b) whether or not the refusal of granting a license of the IP rights will result in adverse effects on competition and innovation in the relevant market, and c) whether or not a grant of license will cause unreasonable damage to the enterprise holding the IP rights.

The industry has shown serious concern regarding Article 7, it is feared that the restriction of IP rights enforcement by the Chinese Essential Facilitiesdoctrine could reduce the incentive to future development of technology in the R&D market[31]. Also, the criterion 'c) whether or not grant of license will cause unreasonable damage to the enterprise holding the IP rights' has come under criticism. Critics insist that long-term damage to the IP rights holder, as well as short-term damage, should be fairly considered in the judgement of this criterion[32].

Also, Article 13 of the SAICIP Guideline states that enterprises may not exploit a technological standard, including mandatory requirement by national technical specifications, because of the enforcement of essential IP rights to the technological standard for the purpose of excluding or restricting market competition.
It states that an enterprise maintaining a dominant market position must not take the

---

30.National Development and Reform Commission, *Request for public comments on Antitrust Guidelines for Abuse of IP draft*, 31 Dec.2015 [hereinafter *NDRC Guide*], *available at* https://www.ndrc.gov.cn/hdjl/yjzq/201512/t20151231_1165948.html. State Administration for Industry and Commerce, *Request for public comments on CAMA enforcement on exercise of IP rights*, 4 Feb. 2016 [hereinafter*SAIC Enforcement Guide*], *available at* http://www.gov.cn/xinwen/2016-02/04/content_5039315.htm.

31.Japan Intellectual Property Association, *Opinions on SAIC's Guideline on the Conduct of Excluding and Restricting the Competition through Abuse of IP Rights draft*,10 July 2014 [hereinafter*JIPA Paper 2014*],*available at*http://www.jipa.or.jp/jyohou_hasin/teigen_iken/14/140710_fairtrade_j.pdf.

32.*Id.* at 4.

following acts, without any justifiable reasons, in the development or implementation of a standard: a) intentionally not disclosing, with knowledge of possible adoption of its patent in a standard, information of the patent to standard setting organization, or explicitly waiving the right, and later claiming the patent after the patent becomes mandatory to the standard, and b) refusing other enterprises to exercise its patent, which is essential to a standard, under reasonable licensing terms, allowing exercising of the patent under unfair licensing terms, or tying a license of the patent with other licenses[33].

The industry criticizes the description of 'including mandatory requirement of national technical specifications' in Article 13 of the guideline because this unique condition could cause impediment of future innovation and reduction of incentives to technology development. Since, through this condition, some IP rights related to de-facto standard technology will be unknowingly incorporated in the national technical specifications and restricted by the regulation of Article 13, although owners of those IP rights are not involved in, and unaware of, the national technical specifications setting process[34].

In addition, the industry is concerned that the definition of 'technological standard' in the guideline is not clear. It insists that the definition of 'technological standard' should cover the de-jure standard technology only, and the de-facto standard technology should be excluded from the scope of the guideline[35]. In this regard, the industry emphasizes that a serious negative effect on market competition is unlikely to be caused by refusal of the IP license incorporated in the de-facto standard technology since an enterprise establishes the de-facto standard technology solely for procurement of their own product or service[36]. Also, it should be noted that competition among multiple de-facto standards in the technology marketcan prevent a serious negative impact on market competition.

In conclusion, it is important to remember that restriction of the IP rights enforcement incorporated in the de-facto standard technology could reduce the incentive of future technological development in the R&D market, especially when enterprises are establishing de-facto standard technology for their own product or service with their own R&D effort and investment[37].

33.*Id.*
34.*Id.*
35.*Id.* at 16.
36.*Id.*
37.*Id.* at 3.

2-2-3   CAMC IP Guideline (2017)

After the announcement of the SAICIP Guideline in 2015, an updated Draft of Anti-Monopoly Guidelines on the Abuse of Intellectual Property Rights was published by the Anti-Monopoly Commission of the State Council of China (hereinafter 'CAMCIP Guideline') in March 2017.

Article 15 of the CAMCIP Guideline follows the Chinese Essential Facilitiesapproach employed by the SAIC IP Guideline and restricts the enforcement of IP rights if the IP rights are deemed to be the essential facility for other enterprises' procurement of product or service in the relevant market. More precisely, refusal of license for IP rights which constitute the essential element for the market activity will be regarded as anti-competitive conduct, when there exists no justifiable reason[38].

The anti-competitiveness of the refusal of license for IP rights under Article 15 will be judged by assessing the following factors: a) commitment of license declared by the owner of the IP rights, b) necessity of entering into the relevant market by other enterprises, c) influence to the innovation caused by the refusal of license, d) lack of other enterprises' will or capability of payment of the reasonable license fee, and e) influence to the consumer's interestand public interest caused by the refusal of license for the IP rights[39].

Furthermore, Article 26 of the CAMCIP Guideline provides its specific framework of restriction on enforcement of the SEP incorporated in the de-jure standard technology. The SEP owner's claim of injunction is regarded as the abusive patent enforcement and anti-competitive conduct, in the event that the claim of injunction is used as a tool of forcing the patent implementer to accept unreasonable license terms. This judgment will be made by assessing the following factors: a) the parties' true will expressed and observed in the license negotiations, b) commitment on injunctive relief based on the SEP, c) proposed license terms discussed in the license negotiations, d) influence of injunction to the SEP license negotiation, and e) influence of the injunction

---

38. Article 15 of Anti-Monopoly Commission of the State Council of China, *Draft of Anti-Monopoly Guidelines on the Abuse of Intellectual Property Rights*, 23 Mar. 2017 [hereinafter *CAMC IP Guideline*], *available at* http://fldj.mofcom.gov.cn/article/zcfb/201703/20170302539418.shtml. *See*Gibson Dunn & Crutcher LLP, *Antitrust in China - 2017 Year in Review*,28 Mar. 2018, *available at* https://www.gibsondunn.com/wp-content/uploads/2018/03/antitrust-in-china-2017-year-in-review.pdf.

39. *Id*. After the announcement of request for public comments in 2017 on the CAMC IP Guideline on the Abuse of Intellectual Property which was prepared based on the previous guidelines announced by NDRC, SAIC and other authorities, the Anti-Monopoly Bureau of State Administration for Market Regulation (SAMR) finally made an official announcement, with CAMC's approval, of the Anti-Monopoly Guidelines for Intellectual Property (SAMR IP Guidelines) in January of 2019. The SAMR IP Guideline maintains the same approach of Chinese essential facilities doctrine on refusal of license.*See* Liu et al., China's IP Antitrust Guidelines Released to the Public, 26 Aug. 2020, https://www.chinalawinsight.com/2020/08/articles/antitrust/chinas-ip-antitrust-guidelines-released-to-the-public/, last visited 1 Aug. 2020.

to downstream market competition and consumer interest[40].

2-2-4   Guidelines for Patent Infringement Determination (2017) and Opinions on Strengthening Intellectual Property Trial to Promote the Development of Innovation (2018) by Beijing Higher People's Court

Following its previous announcement in April 2017 of Guidelines for Patent Infringement Determination (2017)[41] which guided the basic framework of restriction on SEP enforcement of a) abuse of patent rights in the case of malicious acquisition of patents, b) obligation of the compliance with the FRANDcommitment and good faith negotiations, and c) denial of the injunctive relief on SEP in the case of a SEP holder's non-compliance with the FRAND commitment, and other principles[42], the Beijing Higher People's Court issued its additional policy statement of Opinions on Strengthening Intellectual Property Trial to Promote the Development of Innovation (hereinafter 'IP and Innovation Opinion')[43].   This policy was prepared to promote Beijing City's technological development, IP dispute resolution, and innovation within industry[44].

The IP and Innovation Opinion suggests the following policy challenges, including SEP enforcement and FRANDlicensing, in the IP practice: a) guaranteeing innovation-driven development strategy, b) strengthening protection and revolution of IP rights, c) creating a sound business environment, d) utilizing the advanced judiciary system, e) improving the IP dispute resolution mechanism, and f) strengthening professional adjudication in IP disputes[45].

More specifically, the court provides several principles regarding SEP enforcement and

---

40.Article 26 of *CAMC IP Guideline.*

41.Beijing Higher People's Court of China, *Guidelines for Patent Infringement Determination,* 27 Apr. 2017 [hereinafter *Beijing Court Guidelines 2017*], *available at* http://www.bjcourt.gov.cn/article/newsDetail.htm;jsessionid=30F877AA2AD9A29AC7247DA0653D192C?NId=150002896&channel=100014003&m=splc, *and* http://bjgy.chinacourt.org/article/detail/2017/04/id/2825609.shtml.

42.Article 126, 149 & 150 of *Beijing Court Guidelines 2017. See* Meyer-Dulheuer MD Legal Patentanwälte PartG mbB, *Beijing: Revised Guidelines for Patent Infringement Determination,* 17 May, 2017, *available at* https://legal-patent.com/unkategorisiert/beijing-revised-guidelines-for-patent-infringement-determination/.

43.*See* Section 1 of *Beijing Court IP and Innovation Opinion 2018.*

44.Beijing Higher People's Court of China, *Opinions on Strengthening Intellectual Property Trial to Promote the Development of Innovation,*20 Sep. 2018[hereinafter *Beijing Court IP and Innovation Opinion 2018*], *available at* http://www.bjcourt.gov.cn/article/newsDetail.htm;jsessionid=30F877AA2AD9A29AC7247DA0653D192C?NId=150002898&channel=100014003&m=splc, *and* http://www.lawinfochina.com/display.aspx?id=a17f1a3da19e6f1ebdfb&lib=law.

45.Section 1 through 6 of *Beijing Court IP and Innovation Opinion 2018.*

FRANDlicensing in Article 12 of the opinion[46].

Firstly, regarding the injunction based on SEP enforcement, the Beijing Higher People's Court insists that the SEP holder's FRANDlicensing commitment shall not automatically deny an injunctive relief based on its SEP, and the injunctive relief claim by the SEP holder will be denied only in the event that the SEP holder's clear negligent act is found in the course of the FRAND licensing negotiation process. In other words, under this 'clear negligent act in FRAND licensing negotiation' approach the SEP holder's positive and willing altitude for FRAND licensing in negotiations is required for a grant of the injunctive relief, and its observable conduct for the agreement of FRAND licensing can be the key factor in judging whether or not the injunction is granted in each case.

The author observes that China's 'clear negligent act in FRANDlicensing negotiation' approach on the SEP enforcement treatment provides the common framework with the 'a willing prospective licensee hoping the FRAND license' approach indicated by the EU court and the Japanese court.

In addition, the opinion states that during the royalty calculation of SEP, the FRANDroyalty should be determined by 'the sufficient evidence enough to prove the reasonableness of SEP holder's offer in its licensing negotiations'. Furthermore, the Beijing Higher People's Court further insists on 'the importance of avoiding possible royalty stacking caused by multiple SEP holders on the same technology'.

We can observe that the Higher People's Court pays proper attention to the European 'Comparable License Approach' through its statement on 'sufficient evidence enough to prove the reasonableness of SEP holder's offer in its licensing negotiations'. Also, it should be clear that the court also cares about the European 'Top-down Approach' through its statement on 'the importance of avoiding possible royalty stacking'.

Finally, it should be noted that the IP and Innovation Opinion has come under some criticism from Chinese lawyers[47]regarding its effect on the public interest and SEP enforcement. The critics point out that the public interest would be harmed by a loss of consumer benefit in the event that SEP enforcement claiming injunction prevents

---

46.Section 12 of *Beijing Court IP and Innovation Opinion 2018* provides as follows: '12. Exploring rules of trial of standard-essential patent cases and promoting the coordinated development of industries. When the decision to issue an injunction is made, whether either party to the negotiation breaches the principle of good faith and is at obvious fault shall be taken into account in priority, and the belief that an injunction need not be issued if the patentee makes fair, reasonable and non-discriminatory promises shall not be had. The calculation of royalties from standard-essential patent licenses shall be supported by sufficient evidence, with market and technological changes and the contribution of patents to the value of products taken into account. The concurrence of patent license royalties shall be prevented. The abuse of market dominance shall be prudentially identified, and the balance of interests shall be taken into account, so as to ensure the coordinated development of all upstream and downstream industry chains. Patentees and exploiters shall be encouraged to reach a licensing agreement through good faith negotiation. Both patent hold-upand patent hold-out shall be prevented' [*available at* http://www.lawinfochina.com/display.aspx?id=a17f1a3da19e6f1ebdfb&lib=law].

47.*IIP SEP Report H30* at 103-104.

manufacture or sales of products implementing the SEP incorporated in standardized technology. Thus, it strongly emphasizes the necessity of considering the possible impact on public interest caused by SEP enforcement.

However, we should remember that such excessive emphasis on the protection of the public interest could lead to an excessive restriction of SEP enforcement, and it is a serious risk to future promotion of the innovation and incentive to technological development. Regarding this discussion, the author finds that the criticism given by Chinese lawyers has commonality with the Japan Fair Trade Commission study group's statement[48] on the public interest and SEP enforcement as a part of the Japanese Essential Facilitiesdoctrine's discussion in 2003. We should pay careful attention to further discussion regarding the public interest and SEP enforcement, which could lead to an excessive restriction on SEP enforcement in the market, in both China and Japan[49].

2-2-5 Study of China Patents Act Reform for Punitive Damage System (2018-2020)

The National People's Congress committee of China announced its reform plan of Chinese Patents Law, the Draft Amendment of the China Patent Law, which includes a new punitive damages system for willful infringement of patents[50], in December 2018. Since the SEP is supposed to be publicly announced to its implementer in a course of the de-jure standard setting process, the court will be likely to affirm the punitive damages to those SEP infringements.

It is expected that the committee makes a reform of Patents law allowing five times larger amount of damages, at maximum,than the amount of actual damages on willful patent infringers. However, the industry has suggested that the punitive damages system can be abused by Non-Practicing Entities ('NPE') under the Chinese Patent Law's automatic injunctive relief system[51] based on its Civil Law framework[52].

The author observes that China's study of the punitive damages policy is following and responding to the above-mentioned Korean policy discussion on its new punitive

---

48.*JFTC AMA Report 2003.*

49.*Cf.* Endo, *Chugoku ni okeru gijutu hyoujun to tokkyo wo meguru saishin doukou to nihon kigyou nosenryaku (Situation of technology standard and patents in China and strategy of Japanese companies),* 62-64 & 84-95 (2018).Also *see,* as for the essential facilities doctrine and IP in general, Malshe, *Essential Facilities: de facto; de jure,* 40 (3) European Competition Law Review 124, 2019.

50.Saegusa & Partners, Snerihou shuuseian dainikai no shingikou ga ippannkoukai sare public comment no boshu kaishi [Start of request for public comments on the second draft of China Patents Act], 6 Jul. 2020,*available at* https://www.saegusa-pat.co.jp/wp/wp-content/uploads/0200706.pdf.

51.*IIP Enforcement Report H22* at iii & 27.

52.*IIP SEP Report H30* at 103.

damages system in 2018. This interaction between Korea and China is an example of the 'regulatory competition' situation in the East Asian region.

Also, it is the author's understanding that the policy study of a new punitive damages system is a counter-reaction to the previous excessive restriction against enforcement of IP rights related to standard technology in those countries. Japan should not carelessly follow the trend of the punitive damages policy in other East Asian countries and get involved in the 'regulatory competition' situation.

Chapter 6

Conclusion :
'Regulatory Competition'
situation in East Asia

The European decisions in the Samsung case (2014) and Huawei vs. ZTE case (2015) had provided, as stated above, a large impact on East Asian countries, accelerating their AMA policy-making on the restriction of enforcement of IP rights incorporated in standard technology. However, their policy-making tends to aggressively react to the enforcement of IP rights, and those policies are providing some aggressive restrictions. We can observe that there exists an influence from their unique interpretation of the European Essential Facilitiesdoctrine which was firstly introduced by the JFTCStudy Report (2003) in Japan.

It is the author's opinion that this aggressive intervention policy involving enforcement of IP rights incorporated in standard technology in the East Asian countries is beyond the scope of the European decisions in the Samsung case and the Huawei vs. ZTE case which focused the restriction on enforcement of SEP for de-jure standard technology[1]. In this regard, we can observe that those aggressive restriction policies on enforcement of IP rights incorporated in de-facto standard technology by the Chinese authorities and the Korean authority can be made in response to the Japanese authority's aggressive restriction policies on the IP rights enforcement in the JFTCStudy Report (2003) and the first JFTC IP Guideline (2007, Revised 2010, 2016). Also, it should be noted that having those aggressive restriction policies in China and Korea, the JFTC maintains its aggressive position even in the latest revision of the IP Guideline in 2016.
The effect of this relationship on the policy-making regarding IP rights enforcement among the East Asian countries should be regarded as the 'Regulatory Competition' situation., i.e., the situation where multiple countries compete with each other for more aggressive regulation policies.

More specifically, we should remark on the unique interpretation of the European Essential Facilitiesdoctrine in the East Asian countries in the context of their restriction of enforcement of IP rights incorporated in standard technology.
The author is concerned that, although the Exceptional Circumstances test, instead of the European Essential Facilities doctrine, developed since the IMS case (2004) has been employed for their regulation of refusal of license for IP rights by the authorities in European countries, the Chinese authorities still maintain the Chinese Essential

---

1.Furthermore, it should be also noted that some European scholarly opinions insist on de-jure standard technology that Huawei v. ZTE case (2015), as well as Unwired Planet v. Huawei case (2017), should have maintained the 'Exceptional Circumstances' test, which has been employed in the refusal of license cases, as apposed to newly employing the Huawei Rule test [See *Goikoetxea 2019* at 69-72 , *Cascón 2016* at 46-49, and *Petit 2013* at 686&719]. The author expects that the court may add some extra criteria derived from the 'Exceptional Circumstances' test to the Huawei Rule test in any marginal case of SEP enforcement where disturbance of market competition caused by the refusal of SEP license is not very clear. Also, the author believes that JFTC should employ an additional criteria of 'complete elimination of the competition in the downstream market' to its 'willing prospective licensee' test for enforcement of FRAND declared SEPs in Section 4-2-4 [Unfair Trade Practices] of JFTC IP Guideline.

Facilitiesdoctrine approach in their guidelines, and the Japanese authority's position on this matter is not clear in the Section 4-2-iii ('Discriminatory License of Standard Technology' regulation) of the JFTCIP Guideline and has possibly been influenced by the proposed Japanese Essential Facilities doctrine in the JFTC Study Report (2003)[2].

Also, the author observes that those aggressive policies under the AMA which restrict patent enforcement in view of the pro-competition policy have been indirectly leading to further reaction of the discussions on new 'punitive damages system' for patents infringement under the Patents Law, as its antithesis or compensation in view of the pro-patent policy, in Korea, China and Japan since 2019.

Based on the understanding in the above, it is the author's opinion that the AMA authorities in those East Asian countries should clearly describe the requirement of the four examination factors in the 'Exceptional Circumstances test', i.e., a) refusal is blocking the emergence of a 'new product', b) provision of the protected material is 'indispensable', c) competition in the downstream market will be excluded by the refusal, and d) there existed no justification for the refusal, for their restriction on enforcement of the IP rights incorporated in de-facto standard technology in a future revision of their guidelines.

In summary, the author concludes that, in order to avoid any negative effect to technological innovation and future incentive to technology development, the AMA authorities in East Asian countries should promptly make a further revision, especially in terms with a treatment of de-facto standard technology, to their guidelines and clearly limit the outline of their regulation policy for restriction of enforcement of IP rights incorporated in standard technology. The 'Regulatory Competition' situation should be decelerated in those East Asian countries.

2.In contrast, it should be noted that the Korean authority has revised its guideline for deleting the languages of 'essential facility' and 'de-facto standard' in the latest revision of KFTC IP Guideline (2009, Revised 2016) in 2016.

APPENDIX A
JFTC IP Guideline

Guidelines for the Use of Intellectual Property under the Antimonopoly Act
(https://www.jftc.go.jp/en/legislation_gls/imonopoly_guidelines_files/IPGL_Frand.pdf)
Tentative translation

Table of Contents

      (b) Limiting the license period

      (c) Limiting the field where the technology may be used

    (ii) Restrictions pertaining to manufacturing

      (a) Limiting the area in which manufacturing is allowed

      (b) Limiting the quantity of products or the number of times of using the technology in manufacturing

    (iii) Restrictions pertaining to export

    (iv) Sublicensing

(4) Imposing Restrictions in relation to the Use of Technology

    (i) Restrictions on raw materials and components

    (ii) Restrictions on sales

    (iii) Restrictions on selling and resale prices

    (iv) Restrictions on manufacturing and sale of competing products or on transactions with competitors

    (v) Best effort obligations

    (vi) Obligations to protect confidentiality of knowhow

    (vii) No-contest obligation

(5) Imposing Other Restrictions

    (i) Unilateral termination provisions

    (ii) Establishment of royalties without relation to the use of technology

    (iii) Restrictions after extinction of rights

    (iv) Package licensing

    (v) Addition of functions to technology

    (vi) Obligations of the non-assertion of rights

    (vii) Restrictions on research and development activities

    (viii) Obligations to assign improved technology or to grant exclusive licenses for improved technology

    (ix) Obligations to grant non-exclusive licenses for improved technology

    (x) Obligations to report obtained knowledge and experience

Part 1 Introduction

(1) Competition Policy and Intellectual Property Systems

The legal frameworks to protect intellectual property[1] in relation to technology

---

1. Under the Intellectual Property Basic Act, intellectual property is defined as "inventions, devices, new varieties of plants, designs, works and other property that is produced through creative activities by human beings (including discovered or solved laws of nature or natural phenomena that are industrially applicable), trademarks, trade names and other marks that

(hereinafter referred to as "intellectual property systems") may encourage entrepreneurs to conduct research and development and may serve as a driving force for creating new technologies and products based on the
technologies. They can be seen as having pro-competitive effects. In addition,
technology transactions assist in promoting competition by enabling increased efficiency in the use of technology through combinations of different technologies, the formation of new markets for technologies and their associated products, as well as an increase of competing parties. In a free market economy, intellectual property systems motivate entrepreneurs to actualize their creative efforts and contribute to the development of the national economy. It is important to ensure that their basic purposes are respected and that technologies are traded without impedance.

Under intellectual property systems, however, competition in technologies and products may be diminished if a right-holder does not allow other entrepreneurs to use its technology or grants other entrepreneurs a license to use the technology on the condition that their research and development, production, sales or any other business activities are restricted ("restrictions pertaining to the use of technology"), depending on how such refusal or restrictions are imposed and the specific conduct to which the restrictions apply.

Consequently, when applying the Antimonopoly Act with respect to the
restrictions pertaining to the use of technology, it is important for competition policy to insulate competition in technologies and products from any negative effect caused by any restrictions that deviate from the intent of the intellectual property systems, while making every effort to facilitate competition through the intellectual property systems.

Generally intellectual property is not confined to that relating to technology.
However, the Guidelines deal solely with intellectual property concerned with technology.

(2) Scope of Application of the Guidelines

The Guidelines have application to those intellectual properties that are concerned with technology. They are meant to comprehensively specify the principles by which the Antimonopoly Act is applied to restrictions pertaining to the use of technology.

(i) As used in the Guidelines, "technology" refers to any technology protected under the Patent Act, the Utility Model Act, the Act Concerning the Circuit Layout of a Semiconductor Integrated Circuit, the Plant Variety Protection and Seed Act, the

---

are used to indicate goods or services in business activities, and trade secrets and other technical or business information that is useful for business activities" (in Article 2, paragraph (1)).

Copyright Act and the Design Act[2] and to any technology protected as know-how[3]. From the legal point of view, the use of such technology is identical to the use of intellectual property relating thereto. The use of technology is hereinafter used as an expression synonymous with the use of intellectual property.

It generally corresponds to those trade secrets under the Unfair Competition Prevention Act which are concerned with technology. Given that know-how is not given any monopolistic or exclusive right by any specific act, it is characterized, in comparison to what is protected by patent and other rights, by an unclear scope of technology subject to protection, poor exclusiveness of protection and uncertainty concerning the protection period.

(ii) The restrictions pertaining to the use of technology subject to the Guidelines by the right-holder to the technology include (i) any conduct of inhibiting any other party from using the technology, (ii) any conduct of licensing other parties to use the technology within a limited scope and (iii) any conduct of imposing restrictions on activities conducted by other parties licensed to use the technology[4] (Note 4).

The restrictions pertaining to the use of technology may involve either the right-holder to the technology alone or other entrepreneurs as well. The rightholder may impose restrictions either directly on the parties wishing to use the technology or indirectly through a third party. These restrictions may either be imposed in the form of restrictive provisions in an agreement or be imposed implicitly.

The Guidelines apply to any conduct that substantially imposes restrictions pertaining to the use of technology, irrespective of its manner or form.

In some cases of licensing, the licensor may grant a licensee the right to sublicense the licensed technology to third parties. Any restrictions imposed by the licensee on such third parties (sublicensees) are treated in the same manner as restrictions imposed by the licensor on licensees.

(iii) Whether the business activities by entrepreneurs are conducted inside or outside Japan, the viewpoints specified in the Guidelines apply, provided that the activities affect the Japanese market.

---

2. The term "technology" used herein covers technology protected as computer program works under the Copyright Act and as design in the form of an article under the Design Act.

3. Technology protected as know-how in the Guidelines refers to any technical knowledge or experience that is not publicly known or any accumulation thereof the economic value of which is independently protected or controlled by entrepreneurs.

4. Note 4: Hereinafter, the conduct of authorizing other parties to use technology (including the conduct of authorizing the use of computer program works) is referred to as "licensing," the party that grants a license as the "licensor" and the party to which the license is granted as the "licensee." The technology that may be used under the license may be referred to as the "licensed technology."

(3) Outline of the Guidelines

Part 2 of the Guidelines explains the basic principles according to which the Antimonopoly Act applies to restrictions pertaining to the use of technology. It is followed by Part 3, where the principles of the Antimonopoly Act are stated from the viewpoint of private monopolization or unreasonable restrictions on trade, and Part 4, where they are stated from the viewpoint of unfair trade practices.

The Illustrative Examples given in Parts 3 and 4 herein are sample cases of violations that have been found in past decisions. They are presented for the purpose of building an understanding of the descriptions herein. The Reference Example describes alleged facts of violation in a case in which the Japan Fair Trade Commission (JFTC) issued a warning. It is presented as a reference With the establishment of these Guidelines, the Guidelines for Patent and Know-how Licensing Agreements under the Antimonopoly Act published on July 30, 1999 are abolished.

Part 2 Basic Principles on Application of the Anti-monopoly Act

(1) The Antimonopoly Act and Intellectual Property Acts

Article 21 of the Antimonopoly Act prescribes: "The provisions of this Act shall not apply to such acts recognizable as the exercise of rights under the Copyright Act, the Patent Act, the Utility Model Act, the Design Act, or the Trademark Act"[5]
. This means that the Antimonopoly Act is applicable to restrictions pertaining to the use of technology that is essentially not considered to be the exercise of rights.

An act by the right-holder to a technology to block other parties from using its technology or to limit the scope of use may seem, on its face, to be an exercise of rights. The provisions of the Antimonopoly Act apply even to this case if it cannot be recognized substantially as an exercise of a right. In other words, any act that may seem to be an exercise of a right cannot be "recognizable as the exercise of the rights" provided for in the aforesaid Article 21, provided that it is found to deviate from or run counter to the intent and objectives of the intellectual property systems, which are, namely, to motivate entrepreneurs to actualize their creative efforts and make use of technology, in view of the intent and manner of the act and its degree of impact on competition.

5.It is understood that the provision of Article 21 of the Antimonopoly Act applies to technology the exclusive use of which is authorized by any act other than that listed in the same article. In the case of technology protected as know-how, no act confers exclusive rights and the aforementioned provision does not apply.

The Antimonopoly Act is applicable to this kind of act[6].

When determining whether or not any specific act is recognizable as an exercise of the right, attention must be paid to the exhaustion of a right. After a party owning the right to technology legally distributed any product based on the technology in the Japanese market at its own discretion, its right is not infringed by any other party trading in the product in the Japanese market. In other words, the patent or other rights have been exhausted. There is no difference, in the principles of application of the Antimonopoly Act, between the cases where the right-holder imposes restrictions on another party that deals in the product that it has distributed at its own will and where a supplier, in general, imposes restrictions on the dealers that deal in its products.

However, given that technology protected as know-how has the characteristics described in Note 3, it will be treated in the same manner as the technology covered by Article 21 of the Antimonopoly Act.

(2) Principles in identifying a market

(i) In evaluating restrictions pertaining to the use of technology in accordance with the Antimonopoly Act, it is considered, as a general rule, which transactions are affected by them. Then the restrictions will be examined to determine whether or not competition is reduced in the market where the transactions take place.

Whether there is a reduction in competition is examined both from the viewpoint of substantial restraint of competition and from the viewpoint mentioned in Part 4-1-(2) within unfair trade practices in this section.

Apart from examining the effect in reducing competition, when examining the effect from the viewpoint of unfair trade practices, it is occasionally vital to examine whether or not the restrictions constitute unfair competition or an infringement of the basis for free competition (See Part 4-1-(3)).

(ii) The conduct of inhibiting the use of technology or licensing with a limited scope of the use of technology has an adverse impact on competition in the market for the technology or of any product (including a service; hereinafter the same shall apply) using it. The conduct of imposing restrictions on the business activities of licensees when licensing a technology affects not only transactions of technology or any product incorporating the technology but transactions of other items as well, such as those of technology and products supplied with the use of the technology or any product incorporating the technology, and those of other technology, components and raw

---

6.Article 10 of the Intellectual Property Basic Act prescribes: "In promoting measures for the creation, protection and exploitation of intellectual property, consideration shall be paid to secure the fair exploitation of intellectual property and public interests and to promote fair and free competition."

materials, or the requisites to manufacture the product using the technology.

When evaluating any restrictions pertaining to the use of technology according to the Antimonopoly Act, it is imperative to identify the market where the technology is traded, where any product incorporating the technology is traded and where other technology and products are traded, and to examine the impact of the restriction on competition, according to the transactions affected by the restrictions affect.

(iii) The method of defining the market of a general product or service is also used to defining the markets where the technology is traded (hereinafter referred to as "technology market") and where any product incorporating the technology is traded (hereinafter referred to as "product market").

Fundamentally, the market is specified in each case from the viewpoint of substitutability to consumers. Trade in technology is not normally subject to transport constraints. Technology is more likely to be diverted from its current usage to other fields of business. Considering these possibilities, the defined technology market may include some fields where the technology is not actually traded. In other cases, however, the market may be defined the one technology provided that it is used by a large number of entrepreneurs in a specific field of business and that it is extremely difficult for them to develop an alternative technology or to switch to any technical substitute.

Restrictions pertaining to the use of technology can affect competition in developing technologies.   No market or trade, however, can be defined for research and development activities by themselves. Therefore the effect on competition in developing technologies should be evaluated by the effect on competition in the trade of future technologies resulting from such activities or products incorporating the technology.

(3) Method of analyzing the effect in reducing competition

Whether or not restrictions pertaining to the use of technology reduce competition in the market is determined by fully considering the nature of the restrictions, how they are imposed, the use of the technology in the business activity and its influence on it, whether or not the parties pertaining to the restrictions are competitors in the market[7], their market positions (such as market share[8]and rank), the overall competitive conditions that prevail in the markets (such as the number of companies competing with the parties concerned, the degree of market concentration, the characteristics and the degree of differentiation of the products involved, distribution channels and difficulty in

---

7.In evaluating this point, consideration is given to whether (i) the parties are competitors before the license is granted, (ii) the parties become competitors if one party grants another the license, (iii) the parties are not competitors even after the license in question is granted.

8.It is thought that in many cases calculation of the market share in the technology market can be substituted by the market share of the product using the technology in question.

entering the market), whether or not there are any reasonable grounds for imposing the restrictions, as well as the effects on incentives of research, development and licensing. In a case in which multiple restrictions are imposed on the use of technology and the restrictions have an influence on the same market, their combined effect on competition in the market is examined. If they have an influence on different markets, it is necessary to examine their effect on competition in each market and then examine the secondary effects on competition in each market to competition in other markets.

If other entrepreneurs grant licenses for an alternative technology, it should also be examined whether or not they are concurrently practicing similar activities.

(4) Cases where restrictions may have major impacts on competition

(i) Acts between competitors

If restrictions pertaining to the use of technology are imposed among competitors, they are more likely to result in evasion of competition among them or more likely to be used to exclude other competitors than restrictions imposed among non-competitors. This type of conduct is thought to have a relatively strong influence on competition.

(ii) Influential technologies

Restrictions pertaining to the use of technology are likely to have a greater effect on competition when the technology is influential than when it is not.

Generally whether or not particular technology is influential is determined, not by the fact that the technology is deemed to be superior, but through a comprehensive consideration of how the technology is used in the product market, whether or not it is difficult to develop any alternative technology or difficult to switch to any technical substitute and the position of the right-holder to the technology in the technology or product market.

For instance, if any technology becomes a de facto standard in the technology or product market, it is likely to be determined as influential.

(5) Cases where restrictions are deemed to have minor effect in reducing competition

In principle, restrictions pertaining to the use of technology are deemed to have a minor effect in reducing competition when the entrepreneurs using the technology subject to the restrictions in the business activity have a share in the product market (hereinafter referred to as "product share" in this section) of 20% or less in total. This is not applicable however to conduct of restricting selling prices, sales quantity, market share, sales territories or customers for the product incorporating the technology[9]or to the conduct of restricting research and development activities or obliging entrepreneurs to assign rights or grant exclusive licenses for improved technology.

The impact of a particular restriction on competition in the technology market is also deemed to have minor effect in reducing competition if the product share is in principle 20% or less in total. Where the product share is unavailable or the product share is found to be not appropriate to determine the effect on the technology market, the effect in reducing competition is considered to be minor provided that there are at least four parties holding rights to alternative technologies available with no outstanding detriment to business activities.

(The viewpoints given in this section are not applicable, however, when restrictions should be examined from the viewpoint mentioned in Part 4-1-(3) below.)

Part 3 Viewpoints from Private Monopolization and Unreasonable Restraint of Trade

With respect to restrictions pertaining to the use of technology, a question is raised as to whether Article 3 (prohibition of private monopolization or unreasonable restraint of trade) or Article 19 (prohibition of unfair trade practices) is applicable.

An infringement of the provision in Article 3 occurs with any conduct that complies with the behavioral criteria described below and that causes, contrary to public interest, a substantial restraint of competition in any particular field of trade. Trade associations violate the provision in Article 8 if they substantially restrict competition in a particular field of trade. (The viewpoint of Article 19 in the Antimonopoly Act is discussed in Part 4.)

On the basis of the principles on identifying the market described in Part 2-2 the particular field of trade is identified according to the scope of influence of the conduct, in the light of the objects, other parties, areas and modes of trade in the technology or product market.

The method of analyzing the effect on competition is as explained in Part 2-3 above, and hereinafter, "substantially restrict competition" refers to establishing, maintaining and strengthening a state of market control[10].

9.Restrictions imposed by the licensor on licensees on the sales quantity and the sales area of the product incorporating the licensed technology are seen to be an exercise of rights to limit the scope of the use of technology. However, if multiple parties mutually impose such restrictions on each other, the activity is not recognizable as an exercise of rights, as is discussed below in Part 3-2.

10.With respect to the meaning of "substantially restraining competition in any particular field of trade" as provided for in Article 2, paragraph (5) of the Antimonopoly Act, there are court rulings that defined it as a state in which there actually appears or at least is going to emerge a situation in which a specific entrepreneur or trade association can control the

(1) Viewpoints from Private Monopolization

Restrictions pertaining to the use of technology will be examined from the viewpoint of applying provisions regarding private monopolization if they "exclude or control the business activities of other entrepreneurs" (Article 2, paragraph (5) of the Antimonopoly Act).

Whether a restriction pertaining to the use of technology is classified as "exclusion" or "control" may not be uniformly determined according to the manner of the conduct. It should be judged specifically by examining the intent and effects of the individual conduct.

Hereinafter, by categorizing the restriction into that of inhibiting the use of technology, limiting the scope of use of technology and imposing conditions for the use of technology, the principle of whether or not the restriction constitutes private monopolization is explained.

(i) Inhibiting the use of technology

Restrictions by the right-holder to a technology such as not to grant a license for the use of the technology to an entrepreneur (including cases where the royalties requested are prohibitively expensive and the licensor's conduct is in effect equivalent to a refusal to license; hereinafter the same shall apply) or to file a lawsuit to seek an injunction against any unlicensed entrepreneur using the technology are seen as an exercise of rights and normally constitutes no problem.

However, if any such restriction is found to deviate from or run counter to the intent and objectives of the intellectual property systems, as mentioned below, it is not recognizable as an exercise of rights. It then constitutes private monopolization if it substantially restrains competition in a particular field of trade.

(a) In a case where entrepreneurs participating in a patent pool (See 2-(1) below) refuse to grant a license to any new entrant or any particular existing entrepreneurs without any reasonable grounds, to hinder it from using the technology, the restriction may fall under the exclusion of business activities of other entrepreneurs.

Illustrative Example
○ Company X and nine other companies engaging in the manufacture of pachinko game machines, and Association Y held a patent and other rights relating to the manufacture of

market by controlling the price, quality, quantity or other conditions freely at its own will to a certain degree as a result of reducing competition in a market (Refer to the ruling of the Tokyo High Court on the Toho-Subaru case on September 19, 1951, and the ruling of the Tokyo High Court on the Toho-Shintoho case on December 7, 1953). It is understood that the expression refers to establishing, maintaining and strengthening the state of market control as depicted by these rulings. (JFTC Decision No.2 of 2004 on March 26, 2007)

pachinko machines. It was difficult to manufacture any such machines without receiving licenses from them. The ten companies commissioned Association Y to manage these rights and restrained any third party from entering the market by refusing to grant licenses. This was found to be a violation of Article 3 of the Antimonopoly Act. (JFTC Recommendation Decision No. 5 of 1997 on August 6, 1997)

(b) Where a technology is found to be influential in a particular product market and is actually used by numerous entrepreneurs in their business activities, it may fall under the exclusion of business activities of other entrepreneurs if any one of the entrepreneurs obtains the rights to the technology from the right-holder and refuses to license the technology to others, preventing them from using it. (Interception)
For instance, this could apply to a case in which a number of entrepreneurs participate in a patent pool and accept licenses from the pool administrator to use technologies that are essential to their business activities in a particular product market and some of the entrepreneurs in the pool purchase a pooled technology from the pool administrator without notifying other participants to block other participants in the pool from using the technology in their business activities.

(c) In a case in which an entrepreneur conducting business activities in a particular technology or product market collects all of the rights to a technology that may be used by its actual or potential competitors but not for its own use and refuses to license them to prevent the competitors from using the technology, this activity may fall under the exclusion of business activities of other entrepreneurs. (Concentration of rights)
An example might be a situation in which technology A and technology B are alternatives in a product market and the right-holder to technology A and the right-holder to technology B are competing with each other to make their technology the de facto standard, and the right-holder of technology A purchases the rights to a technology that is essential only for the use of technology B but not required for the use of technology A and then refuses to license to any entrepreneur using technology B to conduct its business activities in the product market.

(d) Under the circumstances in which a product standard has been jointly established by several entrepreneurs, it may fall under the exclusion of the business activities of other entrepreneurs when the right-holder refuses to grant licenses so as to block any development or manufacture of any product compliant with a standard, after pushing for establishment of that standard, which employs a technology of the right-holder, through deceptive means, such as falsification of the licensing conditions applicable in the event the technology is incorporated into the standard, thereby obliging other entrepreneurs to receive a license to use the technology.

This also applies in a case in which an entrepreneur holding rights to a technology refuses to grant licenses so as to prevent other entrepreneurs from participating in the bidding after deceiving a public institution into setting out specifications of the product it will be purchasing through bidding that can be satisfied solely by the use of the technology, thereby creating a situation in which no bidder can manufacture any product meeting the specifications without receiving the license to use the technology.

(e) The standard setting organization or trade association (hereinafter referred to as the "SSO") generally makes the document (IPR Policy) describing principles for license of patents (including the other intellectual property rights) essential for implementation of the standards (hereinafter referred to as the "Standard Essential Patent"). It is specified in IPR Policy that, in order to prevent exercise of right in respect of Standard Essential Patents from impeding research & development, production or sale of the products adopting the standards and to broadly diffuse the standards, it makes the participants in standard setting clearly show whether they hold any Standard Essential Patents and their intention for licensing for fair, reasonable and nondiscriminatory conditions (such conditions are generally called "FRAND conditions"). A Standard Essential Patent holder's declaration in writing to show that it is willing to grant licenses under FRAND conditions to the SSO is generally referred to as the "FRAND Declaration". According to the IPR policy, the SSO will study change of the standards to exclude the technology protected by such if such declaration is not made. Since FRAND Declaration makes it possible for the Standard Essential Patent holders to receive reasonable compensation for the use of the Standard Essential Patent and also makes it possible for those who research & develop, produce or sell the products adopting the standards to access Standard Essential Patents under FRAND conditions, FRAND Declarations promote research and development investment of the technologies concerning the standards and also promote positive investments required for research & development, production or sale of the products adopting the standards.

Refusal to license or bringing an action for injunction against a party who is willing to take a license by a FRAND-encumbered Standard Essential Patent holder, or refusal to license or bringing an action for injunction against a party who is willing to take a license by a FRAND-encumbered Standard Essential Patent holder after the withdrawal of the FRAND Declaration for that Standard Essential Patent may fall under the exclusion of business activities of other entrepreneurs by making it difficult to research & develop, produce or sell the products adopting the standards.

The description above shall be applied no matter whether the act is taken by the party which made the FRAND Declaration or by the party which took over FRAND-encumbered Standard Essential Patent or is entrusted to manage the FRAND-encumbered Standard Essential Patent. (The same holds for the case described in Part4-(2), (iv).)

Whether a party is a "willing licensee (who willing to take a license on FRAND terms)" or not should be judged based on the situation of each case in light of the behavior of the both sides in licensing negotiations etc. (For example, the presence or absence of the presentation of the infringement designating the patent and specifying the way in which it has been infringed, the presence or absence of the offer for a license on the conditions specifying its reasonable base, the correspondence attitude to the offers such as prompt and reasonable counter offers and whether or not the parties undertake licensing negotiations in good faith in light of the normal business practices.) Even if a party which intends to be licensed challenges dispute validity, essentiality or possible infringement of the Standard Essential Patent, the fact itself should not be considered as grounds to deny that the party is a "willing licensee" as long as the party undertakes licensing negotiations in good faith in light of the normal business practices.

(ii) Limiting the scope of the use of technology

When a right-holder to a technology grants other entrepreneurs a license to use the technology within a limited scope, it is seen as an exercise of rights and normally constitutes no problem. However, any acts of specifying and enforcing the scope within which the use of technology is authorized (See Part 4-3 for specific details of such conduct) could be deemed acts of controlling the business activities of licensees. As a result of examination according to the principle stated in Part 2-1, if it is found to deviate from the intent of the intellectual property systems, etc., it is not recognizable as an exercise of rights. It then constitutes private monopolization if it substantially restrains competition in a particular field of trade.

(iii) Imposing conditions on the use of technology

When the right-holder to a technology sets a condition for granting a license for the technology to other entrepreneurs, it may correspond to an act of controlling the business activities of licensees or of excluding the business activities of other entrepreneurs, depending on the particular circumstances. If it causes a substantial restraint of competition in a particular field of trade, it will be deemed to constitute private monopolization.

(a) When the right-holder to a technology implements a multiple licensing scheme (see 2-(2) below) for entrepreneurs wishing to conduct business activities using the technology and issues instructions that must be followed by the licensees on selling price, sales quantity, customers and other factors concerning the products supplied with the use of the technology, the holder may be found to have committed an act of controlling the business activities of these entrepreneurs.

Reference Example

○ The production of Product A. To adjust the demand-supply relationship and stabilize the market by controlling the output of the product from the associhe production of Product A. To adjust the demand-supply relationship and stabilize the market by controlling the output of the product from the association members, Association X as a means stipulated in the normal licensing agreement with the members that production quantities shall be determined by the local assembly and approved by the board of directors and that the Association may terminate the agreement with any licensee that has produced more than the predetermined quantity. Association X was found to have enforced these provisions, and the activity was recognized as possibly violating the provision in Article 8 of the Antimonopoly Act. (Warning issued on February 17, 1994)

(b) When the right-holder to a technology concerned with product standards or the technology essential for business activities in the technology or product market ("essential technology") prohibits the development of any alternative technology when granting a license to other entrepreneurs, it corresponds in principle to the act of controlling the business activities of licensees.

Preventing licensees from adopting alternative technology corresponds in principle to the act of excluding business activities of other entrepreneurs[11].

(c) When the right-holder to essential technology imposes an obligation to obtain a license on any technology other than that concerned or to purchase any product designated by the licensor without reasonable grounds when granting a license to other entrepreneurs, it may constitute an act of controlling the business activities of the licensees or the act of excluding the business activities of other entrepreneurs.

(2) Viewpoints from Unreasonable Restraint of Trade

Restrictions pertaining to the use of technology will be examined from the viewpoint of applying the provision regarding unreasonable restraint of trade if "an entrepreneur in concert with other entrepreneurs, colludes to restrict or engage in their business activities" (Article 2, paragraph (6) of the Antimonopoly Act).

It is necessary to examine this from the viewpoint of unreasonable restraint of trade especially in the situation in which the parties involved in the restrictions pertaining

---

11.This is not limited to any conduct of explicitly preventing licensees from developing or adopting alternative technology. It also applies to any case of substantially limiting the development of alternative technology or the like, for instance, by establishing extremely advantageous conditions only to those that refrain from developing the alternative technology.

to the use of technology compete. Possible examples include a patent pool and cross licensing among competitors and a multiple licensing scheme under which numerous competitors are licensees of the same technology.

(i) Patent pool

(a) A patent pool refers to a business activity in which multiple parties holding the rights to a certain technology concentrate their rights individually or the rights to license the technology in a particular corporation or organization so that the body may grant the necessary licenses to the members of the pool or others. The form of corporation or organization varies: it may be set up specifically for the purpose or an existing body may be appointed to fulfill this role. A patent pool can be useful in encouraging the effective use of technologies required for business activities and a patent pool itself does not immediately constitute an unreasonable restraint of trade. For (patent pools formed for standardization, refer to the Guidelines on Standardization and Patent Pool Arrangements published on June 29, 2005.)

(b) Notwithstanding the above, it is an unreasonable restraint of trade if the parties holding the rights to the substitute technologies in a particular technology market establish a patent pool and jointly set forth licensing conditions (including the scope of use of technologies) for their rights to substitute technologies and substantially restrain competition in the field of trade associated with these technologies.
When these entrepreneurs collude to restrict any improvement to the technology licensed to the pool or restrict the licensees, it is an unreasonable restraint of trade if it substantially restrains competition in the field of trade associated with the technology.

(c) When entrepreneurs that compete with one another in a particular product market establish a patent pool for the mutually use technologies required to supply their product and obtain licenses for these technologies from it, their conduct to jointly determine the price, quantity or customers of their products using the licensed technology is an unreasonable restraint of trade if the conduct substantially restrains competition in the field of trade of the product in question.

(d) In a case in which entrepreneurs competing with one another in a particular product market establish a patent pool for technologies required to supply their product as a sole body that can grant licenses to other entrepreneurs, its refusal to grant licenses to new entrants or certain existing entrepreneurs without reasonable grounds constitutes conduct of jointly impeding new entries or hampering the business activities of the existing entrepreneurs. It is an unreasonable restraint of trade if this conduct substantially restrains competition in the field of trade of the product in question.

(ii) Multiple licensing

Multiple licensing refers to a system for granting multiple entrepreneurs licenses to use a technology.

Under the multiple licensing scheme, restrictions on the scope of the use of technology, and selling price, sales quantity, customers or the like with respect to the product manufactured using the technology with the mutual recognition that the licensor and licensees are subject to common restrictions correspond to mutual restraint of the business activities of these entrepreneurs. It is an unreasonable restraint of trade if it substantially restricts competition in the field of trade associated with the product. In addition, by applying the same principle, imposing restrictions on licensees with respect to a technology resulting from research for the improvement or application of the technology hereinafter referred (to as "improved technology") or the adoption of an alternative technology is also an unreasonable restraint of trade if it substantially restrains competition in the field of trade associated with the technology.

Illustrative Example

○ With regard to iron covers for public sewerage systems to be purchased by a local public entity, specifications that incorporate Company X's utility model were adopted on the condition that the utility model would be licensed to other entrepreneurs. Company X granted the license to six other companies. However, it prescribed that the price estimate for iron covers submitted by the six companies to the local government should be equivalent to or higher than that of Company X, that the price at which the covers are supplied by Company X and the six companies to manufacturers and the margin for the manufacturers should be fixed and that Company X should secure a 20% share of the sales quantity with the remainder divided equally among Company X and the six companies. These and other forms of conduct were found to be in violation of Article 3 of the Antimonopoly Act. (JFTC Decision No. 2 of 1991 on September 10, 1993)

(iii) Cross-licensing

(a) Cross-licensing refers to a business activity in which multiple parties that own rights to technology mutually license their rights to one another.

Generally cross-licensing involves fewer entrepreneurs compared to the number of the entrepreneurs participating in a patent pool or in multiple licensing.

(b) Even if the number of entrepreneurs involved is small, cross-licensing may produce similar effects as those caused by the patent pool when it includes joint arrangements on the price, quantity, customers or the like or on not granting the license to others in a situation and where the participating entrepreneurs collectively hold a high share of the market for a particular product. For these reasons, as in (1) above, it constitutes an unreasonable restraint of trade if it substantially restrains competition in the field of trade of the product in question.

(c) It constitutes an unreasonable restraint of trade to set forth jointly each party's scope of the use of technology, which is equivalent to a restriction on the scope of the business activities using the technology, if it substantially restrains competition in the field of trade relating to the technology or product.

Part 4 Viewpoints from Unfair Trade Practices

(1) Basic Viewpoints

(i) Restrictions pertaining to the use of technology are examined not merely from the perspective of private monopolization and unreasonable restraint of trade, but from that of unfair trade practices as well.
The following discusses whether or not restrictions pertaining to the use of technology constitute an unfair trade practice. For convenience, restrictions pertaining to the use of technology are classified into four different types: (i) inhibiting the use of technology, (ii) limiting the scope of the use of technology, (iii) imposing restrictions in relation to the use of technology, and (iv) imposing other restrictions.

(ii) From the viewpoint of applying unfair trade practices, restrictions pertaining to the use of technology will be examined to determine if they comply with certain behavioral criteria and tend to impede fair competition ("tendency to impede fair competition"). With respect to the type of tendency to impede fair competition, the Guidelines focus on what can be judged from the following criteria in accordance with the method of analyzing the effect of reducing competition mentioned in Part 2-3. For other types of tendencies to impede fair competition, refer to (3) below.
(i) Whether or not an entrepreneur (including any entrepreneurs that have a close relationship with it; hereinafter the same shall apply) may deprive its competitors and other parties of trading opportunities or directly impede the ability of the competitors and the others to compete.
(ii) Whether or not the restriction may reduce competition in pricing, acquiring customers and other means.

In this event, with regard to criterion (i), the impact on competition should be judged by specifically considering factors such as the number of entrepreneurs subject to the restriction and the level of competition between the entrepreneurs.

With regard to criterion (ii) the degree of effectiveness of the restrictions should be considered.

When examining criteria (i) and (ii), it is not the case that the restriction meets the criteria only if it causes a tangible effect in reducing competition.

(iii) Apart from criteria (i) and (ii), whether or not the conduct constitutes unfair competition or an infringement of the basis for free competition must in some cases be examined with regard to the tendency to impede fair competition. In this event, judgement should be made by an overall consideration of the details and degree of influence on the licensees' business activities, the number of other parties engaged in the conduct and the duration or repetitiveness of the conduct, etc.

The viewpoint stated in Part 2-5 is not applicable to the examination from these perspectives:

(a) Whether or not the conduct constitutes unfair competition is questioned in a transaction involving technology in relation to the act of deliberately causing misunderstanding of the function or effect of the technology or the details of the rights to the same, the act of disseminating any defamatory information about the technologies of competitors and the act of interfering with competitors' business activities by filing a vexatious lawsuit for an injunction to prevent an infringement of rights, knowing that the rights are invalid (Paragraphs (8), (9) and (15) of the General Designation).

(b) A question over an infringement of the basis of free competition is studied mainly for the unjustifiable imposition of disadvantageous conditions on licensees when granting them licenses in a situation in which the licensor enjoys a dominant bargaining position with respect to the licensees(Paragraphs (10) and (14) of the General Designation).

With respect to the types of activity discussed in 2 to 5 below, besides examining whether or not it tends to impede fair competition (tendency to reduce competition) mentioned in (2) above, depending on individual cases, whether or not the activity breaches the basis of free competition may be examined.

Whether or not the licensor has a dominant bargaining position over licensees is examined through a comprehensive consideration of the degree of influence of the technology (see Part 2-4-(2) above), the extent to which the licensees' business activities depend on the technology, the positions of the parties in the technology or product market, the state of the technology or product market and the disparity in the scale of business activities between the parties.

(iv) The following discussion focuses on whether or not individual restrictions tend to impede fair competition (tendency to reduce competition) as mentioned in (2) above. Applicable paragraphs of the General Designation of Unfair Trade Practices are noted as supplements in the context of the conduct described below. It is not suggested, however, that the applicable paragraphs are limited to those shown, but that they are presumed to be chiefly applied

(2) Inhibiting the Use of Technology

When the right-holder to a technology refuses to grant a license to use the technology to any other entrepreneur or files a lawsuit for an injunction against any unlicensed entrepreneur using the technology to prevent the infringement of the right, the conduct is normally seen as an exercise of the right. According to the viewpoint explained in Part 2-1 above, however, the following conduct is not recognizable as an exercise of the right but are examined whether or not they constitute unfair trade practices.

(i) In a case where an entrepreneur acquires the rights to a technology from the right-holder, with the recognition that a competitor uses the licensed technology in its business activities and that it is difficult for the competitor to replace the technology with an alternative, and the entrepreneur refuses to grant a license for it in order to block the competitor from using the technology, this conduct impedes the use of the technology with the intent of interfering with the competitor's business activities. It is found to deviate from or run counter to the intents and objectives of the intellectual property systems. It is therefore considered to constitute an unfair trade practice if it degrades the competitive function of the competitor and tends to impede fair competition. (Paragraphs (2) and (15) of the General Designation)
For example, if any of the licensees of a technology used by several entrepreneurs as a basis for their business activities in the product market obtains the rights from the right-holder to the technology in order to block competitors (other licensees) from using the technology by refusing to license it to them, this conduct may constitute an unfair trade practice.

(ii) When the right-holder to a technology refuses to grant a license to stop other entrepreneurs from using its technology after urging them to use its technology in their business activities through unjustifiable means, such as falsification of licensing conditions, and making it difficult for them to shift to other technology, the conduct unjustifiably creates the status of an infringement on rights and is found to deviate from or run counter to the intents and objectives of the intellectual property systems. Such conduct constitutes an unfair trade practice if it degrades the competitive function of the other entrepreneurs and tends to impede fair competition. (Paragraphs (2) and (15) of the General Designation)

A sample case that may constitute an unfair trade practice is one in which one of the entrepreneurs engaging in the joint formulation of standards vows to grant a license with extremely advantageous conditions so as to make its technology the basis for a standard and then refuses to grant a license to use the technology to other entrepreneurs after seeing the standard has been established and it has become difficult for the entrepreneurs to shift to another technology.

(iii) In a case where the technology provides the basis for business activities in a particular product market and a number of entrepreneurs, accepting licenses for the technology from the right-holder, engage in business activities in the product market, the conduct of discriminately refusing to license a particular entrepreneur without reasonable grounds is found to deviate from or run counter to the intent and objectives of the intellectual property systems. If such conduct tends to impede fair competition by degrading the competitive function of the entrepreneur in the product market, it constitutes an unfair trade practice[12]. (Paragraph (4) of the General Designation)

(iv) The acts described in Part3-(1), (i), (e), such as refusal to license or bringing an action for injunction against a party who is willing to take a license by a FRAND-encumbered Standard Essential Patent holder, or refusal to license or bringing an action for injunction against a party who is willing to take a license by a FRAND-encumbered Standard Essential Patent holder after the withdrawal of the FRAND declaration for that Standard Essential Patent may deprive the entrepreneurs who research & develop, produce or sell the products adopting the standards of trading opportunities or impede the ability of the entrepreneurs to compete by making it difficult to research & develop, produce or sell the products adopting the standards.

Such acts are considered to be Unfair Trade Practices (Paragraph (2) and (14) of the General Designation) if they tend to impede fair competition, even if the acts do not substantially restrict competition in the product market and are not considered to be Private Monopolization.

The judgement whether a party is a "willing licensee" or not is described in Part3-(1), (i), (e).

12.Restrictive conduct of the kinds mentioned in 3 to 5 below are also examined not only from the perspective of the impacts that they themselves have on competition but also from the perspective of the influence of their discriminatory aspect, if any, on competition.

(3) Limiting the Scope of the Use of Technology

Although an act on the part of the right-holder to the technology of granting other entrepreneurs the license to use a technology within a limited scope, instead of granting a license for unlimited use, may seem, on its face, to be an exercise of rights, in some cases it cannot be recognized substantially as an exercise of rights, as mentioned in Part 2-1 above. Therefore, it is necessary to examine whether this conduct can be recognized as an exercise of rights in accordance with the principles explained in Part 2-1 above. If they are not recognizable as an exercise of rights, they are examined from the viewpoint of unfair trade practices.

(i) Licensing rights in part
(a) Function-specific licensing

When a licensor limits the business activities of licensees using the licensed technology (for example, in the case of patent, the licensor limits the activities, for example, to produce, use, assign or export the technology), it is generally recognizable as an exercise of rights and in principle it does not constitute an unfair trade practice.

(b) Limiting the license period

In principle, when a licensor limits the period during which licensees can use the licensed technology, it does not constitute an unfair trade practice.

(c) Limiting the field where the technology may be used

In principle, when a licensor limits the field in which licensees may engage in business activities using the licensed technology, for example, by limiting the scope of the license to the manufacturing of a specific product, it does not constitute an unfair trade practice.

(ii) Restrictions pertaining to manufacturing
(a) Limiting the area in which manufacturing is allowed

In principle, as in (1) above, when a licensor limits the area in which licensees may use the technology to manufacture products, it does not constitute an unfair trade practice.

(b) Limiting the quantity of products or the number of times the technology is used in manufacturing

In principle, when a licensor imposes a limit on the minimum quantity of products that licensees must manufacture using the technology or the minimum number of times the technology is used, it does not constitute an unfair trade practice provided limiting the minimum number does not eliminate the use of any other technology by the licensees. However, establishing a ceiling on the quantity of products or the number of times within which licensees can use the technology to manufacture products is not recognizable as an exercise of rights if it has the effect of restricting the volume of the products supplied to the overall market. It constitutes an unfair trade practice if it tends to impede fair competition. (Paragraph (13) of the General Designation)

(iii) Restrictions pertaining to export

(a) In principle, when a licensor prohibits licensees from exporting the product incorporating the licensed technology, it does not constitute an unfair trade practice.

(b) In principle, limiting areas to which licensees may export products incorporating the licensed technology will not constitute an unfair trade practice.

(c) The principle discussed in 4-(2)-(a) below applies to judgements made about any limitations on export quantities of the product, if it has the effect of impeding the return of exported products to the domestic market.

(d) Obligations to export via any entrepreneur designated by the licensor are examined in the same manner as restrictions on sales set out in 4-(2)-(b) below.

(e) Limits on export prices are examined in the same manner as mentioned in 4-(3) below where they have an impact on competition in the domestic market.

(iv) Sublicensing

In principle, when a licensor limits parties to which licensees may grant a sublicense, it does not constitute an unfair trade practice.

(4) Imposing Restrictions in relation to the Use of Technology

When the right-holder to a technology licenses other entrepreneurs to use the technology, it may occasionally place restrictions in relation to the licensees' use of the technology for the purpose of realizing the functions or effects of the technology, ensuring safety or preventing any know-how or other confidential information from being divulged or used for unintended purposes. Many such restrictions are considered reasonable to some extent in order to promote the effective use of technology or technology transactions. However, since they restrict the business activities of licensees, they tend to reduce competition in some cases.

Whether or not they have the tendency to impede fair competition must be examined in the light of the question such as whether or not such restrictions are within the extent necessary to meet the aforesaid purposes.

(i) Restrictions on raw materials and components

A licensor may impose limits on licensees as to the quality or suppliers of raw materials, components and other items needed to supply the product using the licensed technology (including services and other technologies; hereinafter collectively referred to as "raw materials and components"). Such limits could be considered necessary to ensure the functions and effect of the technology, to maintain safety and to prevent the disclosure of confidential information and hence are recognized as reasonable to some extent.

However, because the supply of products that incorporate the licensed technology is part of the business activities conducted by licensees, restrictions on raw materials and components have the effect of constraining the means of competition used by licensees or, in other words, the freedom of choosing the quality of raw materials and components and suppliers of them.　They have another effect of depriving the entrepreneurs that supply alternative raw materials and components of trading opportunities.　They therefore constitute an unfair trade practice if they exceed the necessary extent from the above viewpoint and may tend to impede fair competition.　(Paragraphs (10), (11) and (13) of the General Designation)

(ii) Restrictions on sales

In the case in which a licensor sets a limit on the area or quantity in which licensees may sell products (including copies of computer program works) using the licensed technology that applies to the customers or the trademarks that licensees can use, it may constitute restrictions on the licensee's business
activities. (For restrictions on prices, see the following section.)

(a) The stance on limiting the scope of using technology discussed in the first
paragraph of 3 and 3(2) above is basically applicable to limiting the area and
quantity in which products using the licensed technology may be sold.
However, such conduct may constitute an unfair trade practice if the rights are recognized as having been exhausted in Japan or in the case where knowhow is licensed, and there is a tendency to impede fair competition.　(Paragraph (13) of the General Designation)

(b) Unlike the restrictions on the sales area and quantity mentioned in (a) above, placing limitations on the counterparties of the sale of products who may use a licensed technology is not recognized as imposing a limitation on the scope of use of the technology.　It constitutes an unfair trade practice if it tends to impede fair competition.　Examples of this conduct includes limiting counterparties (distributors) to those designated by the licensor, limiting counterparties to those assigned to the licensees and prohibiting sale with specific parties[13]. (Paragraph (13) of the General Designation)

(c) When a licensor imposes on licensees an obligation to use a specific trademark, it is in principle not deemed to constitute an unfair trade practice as this obligation is considered not to tend to reduce competition, except in cases where the trademark is a material means of competition and where licensees are prohibited from using other trademarks as well.

(iii) Restrictions on selling and resale prices

In the case in which a licensor places a restriction on licensees on the selling or resale prices of products incorporating licensed technology, this restriction limits the most fundamental means of competition in the business activities of licensees and distributors purchasing such products from them, and it evidently reduces competition. Therefore it is in principle recognized as constituting an unfair trade practice. (Paragraph (13) of the General Designation)

(iv) Restrictions on the manufacture and sale of competing products or on transactions with competitors

If any licensor imposes a restriction on licensees in relation to the manufacture or selling of any product that competes with the licensor's products or the acquisition of a license for a competing technology from a competitor of the licensor, the conduct has the effect of impeding licensees from effectively using technology and obstructing technology transactions, with the effect of depriving competitors of trading opportunities. Such a restriction therefore constitutes an unfair trade practice if it has the tendency to impede fair competition. (Paragraphs (2), (11) and (13) of the General Designation)

Notwithstanding the above, it is thought that such restrictions to the extent necessary to maintain confidentiality are likely to be recognized as not tending to impede fair competition if the licensed technology is concerned with knowhow and there exists no other means of preventing disclosure or unauthorized use of the technology. This applies also to restrictions that remain effective for a short period after the termination of the agreement.

(v) Best-effort obligations

When a licensor imposes on licensees an obligation to make their best possible efforts

---

13.In a case in which licensees engaging in the production of seeds and seedlings for which variety registrations have been made under the Plant Variety Protection and Seed Act are subject to limitations that requires them to sell their seeds and seedlings only to customers licensed to produce crops from such seeds and seedlings, such limitations are considered requisite to protect the rights concerning crop production from infringement.

in the use of licensed technology, this obligation is regarded as having the effect of ensuring that the licensed technology is effectively utilized. As long as it is confined to an obligation to make an effort, the effect of restricting licensee's business activities is limited and it is unlikely to reduce competition.

Therefore, it does not constitute an unfair trade practice in principle.

(vi) Obligations to protect the confidentiality of know-how

An obligation imposed by the licensor on licensees to protect the confidentiality of licensed know-how during the period of the agreement and after termination of the agreement does not tend to impede fair competition and in principle does not constitute an unfair trade practice.

(vii) No-contest obligation

Imposing an obligation by a licensor on its licensees not to contest the validity of rights for licensed technology[14] is recognized to have aspects to promote competition by facilitating technology transactions and is unlikely to reduce competition directly.

However, it may constitute an unfair trade practices when it is found to tend to impede fair competition by continuing rights that should be invalidated and by restricting the use of the technology associated with the said rights. (Paragraph (13) of the General Designation)

In principle, stipulating termination right of the agreement for the technology with any licensee that challenges the validity of rights may not constitute unfair trade practices.

(5) Imposing Other Restrictions

In addition to those mentioned in 4 above, there are many other restrictions that may be placed on the business activities of licensees on the occasion of granting a license to them.

The following discusses the viewpoints applied to these restrictions.

When it is seen as an exercise of rights that a licensor imposes a particular restriction on licensees, this conduct will be examined in accordance with the principles mentioned in Part 2-1.

(i) Unilateral termination provisions

It is an unfair trade practice to set forth termination terms that are unilaterally

---

14. "Obligation not to contest the validity of rights" refers to, for example, an obligation to agree not to initiate legal action for the invalidation of patents for licensed inventions. It differs from the obligation of non-assertion of rights, detailed in 5-(6) below, which prohibits licensees from exercising any right owned or to be acquired by them against the licensor and other parties.

disadvantageous to licensees in a licensing agreement if the provision is made in combination with any other restrictive activities that infringe the Antimonopoly Act and is used as a means of ensuring the effectiveness of the restrictions. Such terms include, for example, terms that authorize the licensor to terminate the licensing agreement either in a unilateral manner or immediately without allowing for an appropriate grace period. (Paragraphs (2) and (13) of the General Designation)

(ii) Establishment of royalties without relation to the use of technology

When a licensor establishes royalties based on a standard unrelated to the use of the licensed technology, for example by imposing an obligation to pay royalties according to the quantity of products manufactured or sold without the licensed technology, licensees may be hindered from using any competing product or technology. This conduct therefore constitutes an unfair trade practice if it tends to impede fair competition. (Paragraphs (11) and (13) of the General Designation)

In principle, however, it will not constitute an unfair trade practice if the licensed technology is used in part of the manufacturing process or is associated with any component and is reasonable as a means of calculating royalties. For instance, calculating royalties using the manufactured or sales quantity or the value of the final product using licensed technology or components or the quantity of raw materials and components used is recognized as reasonable for the convenience of computation.

(iii) Restrictions after the extinction of rights

When a licensor imposes on a licensee a restriction on the use of a technology or an obligation to pay royalties even after the rights to the technology have become extinct, it generally impedes the free use of technology. It will constitute an unfair trade practice if it tends to impede fair competition. (Paragraph (13) of the General Designation)

Notwithstanding the above, the royalty payment obligation is thought not to unjustifiably restrain licensees' business activities if it is within the permissible extent of an installment or the deferred payment of royalties.

(iv) Package licensing

An obligation imposed by a licensor on licensees to obtain a package license covering a technology other than the technology they wish to use[15][16]is examined based on the same viewpoint as that which applies to restrictions on raw materials and components

---

15.The determination on whether or not any such obligation is imposed depends on whether or not it is substantially difficult for licensees to choose any technology other than that designated by the licensor.

16.Package licensing as discussed in this section does not correspond to the case in which licensees are obliged, under a package licensing agreement for multiple patents and other rights, to pay royalties solely for those patent and other rights that they actually use and not for the other items licensed.

discussed in 4-(1) above, provided, for instance, that it is essential to obtain the effect of the technology sought by licensees or is otherwise recognized as reasonable to some extent.

However, if such an obligation is not essential for ensuring that the licensed technology exerts its effect or if licensees are obliged to obtain a technology license beyond the necessary extent, licensees may be restrained from freely choosing technology and competing technology may be excluded. It therefore constitutes an unfair trade practice if it tends to impede fair competition.   (Paragraphs (10) and (13) of the General Designation)

Illustrative Example

○ Company X imposed on manufacturers and distributors of personal computers (PCs) in trading relations with the company an obligation to (i) additionally preinstall or bundle word processing software unduly under the license to ship PCs preinstalled or bundled with spreadsheet software and to (ii) pre-install or bundle unjustifiably schedule management software under the license to ship PCs preinstalled or bundled with spreadsheet software and word processing software.

Company X was found to be in violation of Article 19 of the Antimonopoly Act (Paragraph (10) of the General Designation). (JFTC Recommendation Decision No. 21 of 1998 on December 14, 1998)

(v) Addition of functions to technology

Granting a license again by a licensor for the use of a technology already licensed but with new functions added is generally identical to a license for improved technology. Therefore this conduct is not immediately recognized as a restriction associated with licensing.

However, let us assume a situation in which a particular technology provides a function whereby other products and services are offered on the basis of the specifications and standards of the technology ("platform function") and where many different applied technologies have been developed on the basis of the platform function to compete with one another. If the licensor of this technology introduces new licensing that incorporates some of the functions supported by the existing applied technologies into its platform function under the circumstances assumed above, the new licensing has the effect of preventing the licensees from using other applied technologies and of depriving other entrepreneurs of the trading opportunities associated with offering the applied technologies, given that licensees have no alternative but to be granted the new license. It therefore constitutes an unfair trade practice if it has the tendency of impeding fair competition. (Paragraphs (10) and (13) of the General Designation)

(vi) Obligations of the non-assertion of rights

When a licensor imposes on licensees an obligation to refrain from exercising, in whole or in part, the rights owned or to be acquired by them against the licensor or any entrepreneurs designated by the licensor[17], this obligation could result in enhancing the influential position of the licensor in a product or technology market or could impede the licensee's incentive to engage in research and development, thereby impeding the development of new technologies by restricting the exercise of the licensee's rights, etc. It therefore is an unfair trade practice if it tends to impede fair competition. (Paragraph (13) of the General Designation)

However, as with the obligation to grant non-exclusive licenses for improved technology as discussed in (9) below, it does not constitute an unfair trade practice in principle if the licensees are, in effect, merely obliged to grant a nonexclusive license for improved technology developed by them.

(vii) Restrictions on research and development activities

Restrictions by the licensor relating to free research and development activities on the part of licensees, such as a provision set forth by the licensor to prohibit licensees from independently or jointly with any third party conducting research and development activities concerning the licensed technology or any technology that competes with it, generally affects research and development competition and ultimately reduces future competition in the technology or product market.

Such restrictions are recognized as having the tendency to impede fair competition[18]and are in principle recognized as an unfair trade practice. (Paragraph (13) of the General Designation)

On the other hand, when the licensed technology is protected and controlled as knowhow, restricting licensees from jointly performing research and development activities with any third party to the extent necessary of preventing disclosure of the knowhow or its use for unauthorized purposes is generally not recognized as having the tendency of impeding fair competition and does not constitute an unfair trade practice.

(viii) Obligations to assign improved technology or to grant exclusive licenses for improved technology

(a) If a licensor imposes on licensees an obligation to hand over to the licensor or any

---

17.This obligation includes an obligation to license the licensor or any entrepreneur designated by the licensor to use the patents and other rights owned or to be acquired by licensees in whole or in part.

18.Generally, a prohibition on modifications to computer program works is seen as an exercise of rights under the Copyright Act. However, licensees are allowed to modify licensed software to use it more effectively under Article 20, paragraph (2), item (iii) and Article 47-2 of the Copyright Act. Restraining such conduct, therefore, is not recognizable as an exercise of rights.

designated entrepreneurs the rights for improved technology developed by them or to grant the licensor an exclusive license for it[19], this conduct enhances the position enjoyed by the licensor in the technology or product market and discourages licensees from working on research and development by obstructing them from using their improved technology.

Normally it is not thought that there is any justifiable reason for instituting such restrictions. In principle, it constitutes an unfair trade practice to impose any such obligation[20]. (Paragraph (13) of the General Designation)

(b) An obligation that forces licensees to co-own the rights for improved technology they invent with the licensor restricts the freedom of use or disposition of the results of the licensees' own improvements or applied research, although the degree to which the obligation discourages them from undertaking research and development activities is less than the restrictions stated in (a) above. It may also constitute an unfair trade practice if it has the tendency to impede fair competition. (Paragraph (13) of the General Designation)

(c) However, in a case in which the improved technology created by a licensee cannot be used without the licensed technology, the obligation imposed on licensees to assign the rights for the improved technology in exchange for fair consideration could be recognized as essential to promote technology transactions. Moreover, it is not recognized as detrimental to the licensees' motivation for research and development. It is generally confirmed to have no tendency to impede fair competition.

(ix) Obligations to grant non-exclusive licenses for improved technology

(a) When a licensor imposes on licensees an obligation to grant the licensor nonexclusive licenses for improved technology attained by licensees, it may not constitute an unfair trade practice in principle as long as the licensees may still freely use their own improved technology. This obligation has little impact on licensees' business activities and is not recognized as being likely to discourage the licensees from undertaking research and development.

(b) However, if the obligation accompanies a limit on the parties that can be licensed to

---

19. As used in the Guidelines, an "exclusive license" includes the exclusive license provided for in the Patent Act and a practice in which the right-holder grants a normal license having an exclusive nature and refrains from exercising its rights in the area covered by the license granted. If the right-holder reserves the right to use the licensed technology on its own, the license is treated as non-exclusive.

20. This restriction does not correspond to the imposition of an obligation on licensees to grant the licensor a right to make applications for a patent or for other rights in the countries and areas where the licensees do not wish to make such an application.

use the improved technology, for instance by imposing an obligation to grant no license to any competitor of the licensor or to any other licensee, it may reduce the motivation of licensees to undertake research and development and possibly enhances the position enjoyed by the licensor in the technology or product market. It therefore constitutes an unfair trade practice if it has the tendency to impede fair competition[21]. (Paragraph (13) of the General Designation)

(x) Obligations to report obtained knowledge and experience

Imposing on licensees an obligation to notify the licensor of knowledge or experience they obtain in the process of using the licensed technology will enhance the incentive for the licensor to offer licenses and will not reduce the motivation of licensees to undertake research and development. It does not therefore constitute an unfair trade practice in principle. However, if imposing an obligation to report knowledge or experience owned by licensees effectively means forcing licensees to grant the licensor a license for their acquired knowhow, it will constitute an unfair trade practice if it has the tendency to impede fair competition according to the viewpoints described in (8) and (9) above. (Paragraph (13) of the General Designation)

21.In a case where the improved technology created by a licensee cannot be used without the technology owned by the licensor, it may in principle not constitute an unfair trade practice to impose an obligation to obtain from the licensor approval for granting a license to any other entrepreneur.

APPENDIX B

JPO SEP License Negotiation Rules

GUIDE TO LICENSING NEGOTIATIONS INVOLVING STANDARD ESSENTIAL PATENTS

(https://www.meti.go.jp/press/2018/06/20180605003/20180605003-2.pdf)

June 5, 2018

Japan Patent Office

TABLE OF CONTENTS

I. Purpose of the Guide

A. SEP Issues and Background

(Changes in Relation to Standards and Patents)

The Guide to Licensing Negotiations involving Standard Essential Patents ("this Guide") aims to enhance transparency and predictability, facilitate negotiations between rights holders and implementers, and help prevent or quickly resolve disputes concerning the licensing of standard essential patents ("SEPs"), which are the patents essential in implementing standards in the field of wireless communications and the like.

While a patent granting exclusive rights to a technology as compensation for disclosing an invention and a standard designed to spread a technology as widely as possible both help to promote innovation, the seeming contradiction between them also often gives rise to tension. That tension first became evident in the 1990s when telecommunications technologies started shifting to digital formats, accompanied by a trend toward standardizing the latest technologies even while protecting them with patents, resulting in SEP disputes.

With respect to SEP disputes, two issues which many are concerned about are "hold-up" and "hold-out," and there is controversy between rights holders and implementers over which of the two is more serious.

"Hold-up" is a situation whereby businesses providing key social infrastructure or services using SEPs that are essential to the operation of those businesses are faced with the threat of injunction. Legal precedents across the world seem to be converging toward permitting injunctions concerning FRANDencumbered SEPs (i.e., SEPs for which a FRAND declaration has been made) only in limited situations. Nevertheless, with courts continuing to grant injunctions, holdup remains an issue for implementers.

On the other hand, rights holders point to the issue of "hold-out," whereby the implementer receives an offer for licensing negotiations from the rights holder, but fails to engage in negotiations in good faith in anticipation that an injunction will be denied on SEPs.

Standards setting organizations ("SSOs") have formulated policies concerning SEPs ("IPR policy") designed to prevent disputes and promote the widespread use of the SEPs necessary for implementing technical standards. Part of this endeavor has included developing policies to ensure that SEP licenses are "fair, reasonable and non-discriminatory" ("FRAND"). This has encouraged companies and other parties participating in standardization to propose high-quality technologies to SSOs and has made a substantial contribution to the widespread adoption of standard technologies.

At the same time, there is a strong call for enhancing transparency in relation to the essentiality and validity of SEPs. Some rights holders might deliberately overdeclare their patents as SEPs to SSOs when they are not actually essential, and in any event, it is normal to declare patents as essential when they are still in the application phase and when the standard is not itself settled. A certain amount of overdeclaration is therefore inevitable, and much better than underdeclaration. Some point out that such overdeclaration has been encouraged by the industry practice of determining royalties at least partly in proportion to the number of SEPs held in relation to a certain standard. SSOs typically do not check whether the patents declared by the rights holder as essential are in fact essential, or whether changes made to technical specifications during the standard creation process have made a patent inessential. In addition, there is no routine third-party review process at the SEP listing stage. (Paradigm Shift in Licensing Negotiations)

The spread of the Internet of Things ("IoT") in recent years has spurred a fourth industrial revolution across the world whereby various types of infrastructure and devices are connected via the Internet, and this trend is transforming licensing negotiations for the SEPs required to implement standards related to wireless communication among devices.

SEP licensing negotiations in the Information and Communication Technology ("ICT") field traditionally took place chiefly among ICT companies.

Therefore, issues were commonly resolved through cross-licensing, and the practice was to conduct negotiations as necessary after the start of a service. In addition, coming from the same industry made it easier for the parties to assess the scope, essentiality, and value of each other's patents, so they tended to share a similar perspective on reasonable license rates.

With the spread of IoT, however, companies from a whole spectrum of different industries have begun using ICT standards, raising the possibility that they too will be brought to the negotiating table. For example, in addition to those telecommunications companies holding SEPs, negotiations may now involve endproduct manufacturers such as automobile makers as well as businesses providing services and infrastructure which do not hold strong SEPs themselves but do need to use them.

Further, there are now cases in which Patent Assertion Entities ("PAEs") that are not engaged in business operations but rather generate revenue solely by asserting patents also become party to negotiations and disputes concerning SEPs.

As the parties to licensing negotiations become more diverse, various aspects of those negotiations too are changing. As noted above, with licensing negotiations now taking place between ICT companies and companies in other industries, it is becoming harder to resolve disputes through cross-licensing. In addition, divergent perspectives on essentiality and licensing rates are fostering unease over SEP-related negotiations and disputes.

(Motivations for Creating this Guide)

With companies from a broad spectrum of industries now finding themselves involved in SEP licensing negotiations, there is a call for appropriate information to be provided to enable businesses not familiar with such negotiations to feel confident taking a seat at the negotiating table.

A considerable body of domestic and international legal precedents has begun to accumulate in relation to SEP disputes, and government agencies around the world are developing guidelines and policy documents[1]. The concept of FRAND royalties too has been examined in a number of legal cases.

It would be useful to analyze these developments and identify elements that should be considered to achieve a balance between the interests of rights holders and implementers with respect to negotiation procedures and methods of calculating royalty rates.

1.In November 2017, the European Commission announced the European Commission Communication on Standard Essential Patent (SEP) Licensing (below, European Communication), urging SSOs to increase SEP transparency and indicating general principles in relation to FRAND licensing terms for SEPs.

B. Nature of this Guide

The SEPs addressed in this Guide are those which the current or original rights holder has presented to an SSO as a FRAND-encumbered SEP.

This Guide is not intended to be prescriptive, is in no way legally binding, and does not forejudge future judicial rulings. It is intended to summarize issues concerning licensing negotiations as objectively as possible based on the current state of court rulings, the judgement of competition authorities, and licensing practices, etc.

While the legal basis for limiting an injunction concerning a FRANDencumbered SEP varies from country to country according to their respective legal systems, in many cases, it seems to have been different factual situations that have led courts in different countries to reach different conclusions. Recent years have seen increasing cross-border convergence in case law as to how parties should behave in SEP licensing negotiations based on the dedication to a factual inquiry into good faith negotiations.

In these circumstances, this Guide aims to offer an explanation of what actions companies can take to make it more likely for them to be recognized as "negotiating in good faith," helping implementers to avoid an injunction and rights holders to secure appropriate compensation. This Guide also discusses how to engage in such negotiations efficiently.

This Guide presents factors to be considered when determining a reasonable royalty, not "recipes" which can be used to automatically calculate an appropriate royalty. In other words, a solution cannot mechanically be produced by simply following this Guide. Given the diversity of SEP licensing negotiations and of the circumstances in which the parties to such negotiations are placed, a solution has to be worked out in each particular case. Not all the issues noted in this Guide will apply to all negotiations. Our hope is therefore that this Guide might be used by qualified experts when advising small and medium enterprises (SMEs) and other parties with limited experience in dealing with SEP issues.

In formulating this Guide, we invited the submission of proposals between September 29 and November 10, 2017, receiving around 50 responses from Japan and abroad. We also called for public comments between March 9 and April 10, 2018, receiving around 50 comments from Japan and abroad. In addition, we engaged in discussions with experts from industry, academia and law, who offered many valuable comments and insights. The content of this Guide owes much to these inputs.

With the environment surrounding SEP licensing negotiations continuing to transform, we plan to review and revise this Guide as appropriate in an open and transparent process so that it continues to evolve and remains "living."

II. Licensing Negotiation Methods

A. Good Faith

Although FRAND means "fair, reasonable and non-discriminatory", there are two aspects to FRAND: (1) the negotiation process itself and (2) the terms of the resulting license. While the purpose of licensing negotiationsis to determine whether a license is necessary, and, if so, the appropriate licensing terms, it is the negotiation process that impacts on whether or not an injunction is justified. Therefore, this chapter will address the first aspect of FRAND.

When patent rights are infringed, rights holders may in principle exercise their right to seek an injunction. When implementers intend to obtain a license on FRAND terms in good faith, however, court decisions around the world are consistent in imposing limitations on granting injunctive relief to owners of FRAND-encumbered SEPs[2]. There are independent and overlapping legal mechanisms by which this is achieved.

One is contracts. The rights holder gives a commitment to the SSO to grant licenses on FRAND terms. In some countries, that commitment, is contractually binding between the SSO and the rights holder, and the contract will be governed by a particular law (e.g. French law in the case of a contract with ETSI[3]). The laws of those countries permit a third party to enforce a contract where it is for the benefit of that party, so a third-party implementer can insist upon a rights holder granting it a license on FRAND terms. If the rights holder does not do so, or does not offer.

FRAND terms, it is in breach of contract, and it will be prevented from enforcing its patent accordingly.

Another is competition law. Where it is found that a rights holder has abused a dominant position, this constitutes a violation of competition law.

There is also a mechanism that draws on the legal principle of the abuse of rights[4].

What, then, is regarded as a demonstration of good faith? While the way in which licensing negotiations are progressed needs to be determined among the parties on a case by case basis and with regard to the laws and rulings of the country or countries in which the patent will be implemented, the 2015 decision by the Court of Justice of

---

2.However, some court rulings have allowed an injunction (St. Lawrence v. Deutsche Telekom and HTC (Germany, district court, 2015), NTT DoCoMo v. HTC (Germany, district court, 2016), St. Lawrence v. Vodafone and HTC (Germany, district court, 2016), Unwired Planet v. Huawei (UK, high court, 2017)).

3.European Telecommunications Standards Institute

4.In Japan, a FRAND declaration made by an SEP rights holder to an SSO is not regarded as a contract for a third-party beneficiary (i.e., an implementer), and the rights holder is regarded as having the obligation to negotiate in good faith with the third party (the implementer) under the principle of good faith prescribed by civil law. If this obligation is not met, the exercise of injunction rights may be restricted as an abuse of rights (Apple v. Samsung (Japan, IP high court, 2014)).

the European Union ("CJEU") in the case between Huawei and ZTE[5]in particular has attracted wide attention. It provided a framework for good faith negotiations between rights holders and implementers by identifying actions which each of the parties should take at each stage of the licensing negotiations. This framework details the rules of negotiations from the perspective of competition law in Europe, and not every court decision in each country follows this framework.

Nevertheless, the framework is considered to be a useful approach in terms of encouraging good faith negotiations whereby rights holders may fulfill their FRAND obligations and implementers may minimize their risk of an injunction, regardless of the differences among jurisdictions in the legal bases for stipulating the negotiation rules for FRAND-encumbered SEPs.

The framework, however, does not provide specific details about negotiations, such as the scope of information that the parties should submit at each stage of the negotiation and the period given to make a response. While some parties regard the lack of specific detail as increasing the flexibility of negotiations, others suggest that it undermines the predictability of licensing negotiations.

Under these circumstances, this Guide has drawn on the framework presented by the CJEU and informed by court decisions in various countries and actual practices in SEP disputes in listing more specific issues relating to actions that parties may take at each stage of licensing negotiations. Framework details should eventually emerge through the accumulation of rulings over the coming years.

It should be noted that simply satisfying the various elements noted in this Guide provides no guarantee of recognition of good faith. Rather, a comprehensive assessment of the negotiating process as a whole needs to be made in each case.

Once again, this Guide is not intended to be prescriptive, and the manner in which negotiations are progressed should be determined among the parties on a case by case basis.

[Steps of the Licensing Negotiation Process][6]

Step 1: Licensing Negotiation Offer from Rights Holder

Step 2: Expression from Implementer of Willingness to Obtain a License

Step 3: Specific Offer from Rights Holder on FRAND Terms

Step 4: Specific Counteroffer from Implementer on FRAND Terms

Step 5: Rejection by Rights Holder of Counteroffer/Settlement of Dispute in Court or through ADR

5.Huawei v. ZTE (EU, CJEU, 2015)

6.The list below is not intended to suggest that each of the five steps is necessarily mandatory in every case. Steps may vary according to the particular case.

1. Step 1: Licensing Negotiation Offer from Rights Holder

(Overview)

In general, if an implementer is suspected to have infringed patent rights, the rights holder may initiate negotiations with the implementer by specifying the relevant patents and identifying how those patents have been or are being infringed[78].

In some cases, an entity that manages a framework enabling patents held by multiple rights holders to be licensed efficiently in a single transaction ("patent pool") may negotiate in place of the rights holder.

It is common for the rights holder to substantiate the infringement by providing to the implementer, among other things[910]:

(1) Documents identifying the SEPs (list of patent numbers[1112], the names of the standards at issue, the geographical scope of patents, etc.); and (2) Documentation mapping claims of the SEPs to the standards and/or products (claim charts[13], etc.).

When a rights holder holds large numbers of SEPs, the parties sometimes discuss limiting the negotiations to key patents so as to rationalize the negotiation process (refer to II.B.4.). (Documentation Mapping Claims of the SEPs to the Standards and/or Products) Rights holders provide documentation to implementers at the start of negotiations so that implementers can see how the SEP claims map to standards and/or their own products. It is common for rights holders to use claim charts to indicate the correlation between products that are actually manufactured and patent claims.

Claim charts may be useful for implementers in analyzing whether they are infringing the SEPs. Meanwhile, by presenting claim charts, the rights holders may demonstrate that they are providing information in good faith to implementers.

When patents are SEPs and the details of patent claims are consistent with standards documents, and if the implementers advertise that their products conform to the

---

7.The framework in Huawei v. ZTE (EU, CJEU, 2015) suggests that the rights holder first alerts the alleged infringer of their infringement by identifying the patents and specifying the way they have been infringed.

8.In the field of telecommunications, although implementers often start a negotiation only after receiving an invitation to license from a rights holder, because of the large number of SEPs and/or patentees, it may be useful for parties to refer to the framework of this Guide even if such negotiations are initiated by the implementer before it launches business operations.

9.Besides these, there is a view that rights holders may demonstrate their good faith by, for example, presenting evaluations by third-party experts and examples from past cases, etc.

10.In some cases including where the SEP has a substantial licensing history, the implementer may decide that such substantiation is unnecessary.

11.In NTT DoCoMo v. HTC (Germany, district court, 2016), the court stated that it is necessary to at least indicate the patent number. In Sisvel v. Haier (Germany, high court, 2016), the court stated that it is an industry practice to present 10 to 15 representative patents as a "proud list."

12.In NTT DoCoMo v. HTC (Germany, district court, 2016), the court stated that rights holders need to inform the implementer that the patent is declared standard essential to an SSO.

13.In Sisvel v. Haier (Germany, high court, 2016), the courts stated that at this stage of the licensing procedure, it was not yet necessary to explain the infringement act by providing claim charts. Meanwhile, in NTT DoCoMo v. HTC (Germany, district court, 2016), the courts stated that claim charts based on practices are sufficient for substantiating the infringement.

applicable standards, the act of indicating the correspondence between patent claims and standards may be sufficient. Thus, mapping patent claims to actual products may not always be necessary[14].

Some claim charts explain the connection between claim terminology and the corresponding features of the standards documents or products. In some cases, rights holders may claim that the explanation includes confidential information. In such situations, the parties may conclude a confidentiality agreement (non-disclosure agreement) in licensing negotiations. (Refer to II.B.3.)

While both claims and standards documents are made public and are not in themselves confidential, rights holders tend to require the conclusion of confidentiality agreements as a condition for providing claims charts on the grounds that the correspondence between claim terminology and standards documents and the interpretation thereof constitute confidential information. Implementers, on the other hand, tend to argue that in cases where claim charts only provide a simple comparison between claim terminology and standards documents, the charts do not constitute confidential information and should not be subject to a confidentiality agreement.

If a rights holder demands that an implementer enter into a confidentiality agreement as a condition for providing claim charts even when the rights holder can prepare claim charts that do not include confidential information, this may increase the likelihood of the rights holder being perceived as acting in bad faith. On the other hand, if an implementer demands that a rights holder provide detailed claim charts that do include confidential information while refusing to conclude a confidentiality agreement, this may increase the likelihood of the implementer being perceived as acting in bad faith.

(Documents Demonstrating the Essentiality of SEPs)

When a rights holder and an implementer cannot agree on the essentiality of a patent, they may obtain an analysis from an independent evaluator (an independent company or organization that provides the service of reviewing patents for essentiality). The JPO has a system in which a panel in the Trial and Appeal Department provides an advisory opinion with no legally binding force in relation to the technical scope of a patented invention, and from April 2018 started offering a determination of the essentiality of a patented invention.

Declaration documents, in which rights holders made a FRAND declaration to SSOs, are based on the rights holders' technical assessment that the patents are essential, but not assessment by a neutral third party.

14.In Fujitsu v. Netgear (U.S., CAFC, 2010), the court stated that if an accused product operates in accordance with the standards, then comparing the claims to the standard is the same as comparing the claims to the accused product. The court also stated that if the relevant section of the standard is optional, standards compliance alone would not establish that the accused infringer chooses to implement the optional section.

(Notes on Rights Holders' Actions)

The following are examples of actions by a rights holder that may increase the likelihood of the rights holder being perceived as acting in bad faith:

(1) Demanding injunctive relief before or immediately after sending a warning letter to the implementer, or immediately after opening a negotiation;

(2) Not disclosing its documents identifying the SEPs and documentation mapping SEP claims to the standards and/or products such as claim charts, when offering licensing negotiations to an implementer, such that the implementer can understand the rights holder's claims;

(3) Claiming that it will not provide documentation mapping SEP claims to the standards and/or products such as claim charts to the implementer unless the implementer concludes a confidentiality agreement, even though the documentation does not include confidential information;

(4) Making an offer that sets a time limit that does not allow a reasonable period of time for consideration; or

(5) Not disclosing the content of a portfolio to the implementer (the technologies, number of patents, regions, etc., covered by the portfolio).

Some argue that the information which the rights holder needs to provide additionally so that the implementer can garner the necessary information for negotiations is less extensive in the case of a patent license once granted to the implementer that has since expired than in the case of concluding a new licensing agreement[15][16].

2. Step 2: Expression from Implementer of Willingness to Obtain a License

(Overview)

When an implementer receives an offer from a rights holder for licensing negotiations, it may help to mitigate risk for the implementer not to leave that offer unanswered even if it does not agree with the rights holder's offer, but instead to respond in good faith[17]. After receiving documents including those identifying the SEPs and claim charts from the rights holder, if the implementer concludes that it needs to obtain a license for the SEPs, it may express its willingness to conclude a licensing agreement with (that is, to obtain a license from) the rights holder. Some argue that this willingness should be gauged by the implementer's actions rather than words—in other words, not just the expression of willingness but evidence of this in the way that the implementer

---

15.Unwired Planet v. Huawei (UK, high court, 2017)

16.There is a view, however, that it may require attention because the patent portfolio of the SEP licensor may have changed significantly (e.g., patents have been added to the portfolio or have expired).

17.In Huawei v. ZTE (EU, CJEU, 2015), the court stated that the alleged infringer should diligently respond to the SEP holder's offer, in accordance with recognized commercial practices in the field and in good faith, this being a matter that must be established on the basis of objective factors and which implies, in particular, that there are no delaying tactics.

approaches negotiations.

Some hold the view that, when an implementer receives an offer from a rights holder for licensing negotiations, the implementer should promptly express its willingness to obtain a license even if discussions are still being conducted about essentiality, validity, and infringement, reserving the right to challenge these issues.

Others take the view, however, that parties should first conduct discussions about essentiality, validity, and infringement before the implementer expresses its willingness to obtain a license.

(Countermeasures by Implementers)

In practice, a rights holder and an implementer in licensing negotiations may not see eye-to-eye, and may fail to reach an agreement on essentiality, validity or infringement. In such cases, the implementer can express its willingness to obtain a license without waiving its right to challenge these issues[18][19].

An implementer may still challenge, for example, the following issues on patent rights for which it intends to obtain a license:

(1) Whether the patents are truly essential;

(2) Whether the patents are valid;

(3) Whether the implementer has infringed these patents;

(4) Whether the patents are enforceable[20];

(5) Whether the entity who has exercised its rights is the true holder of the patents; and

(6) Whether the patents have not been exhausted.

When implementers challenge the issues identified above, they may be required to provide specific grounds of such positions. For example, it is useful for them to provide, among other things:

(1) Documents that provide the basis for the implementers' refutation that they do not infringe the subject patents;

(2) Prior art that serves as grounds for invalidating the patents;

(3) Technical information that provides the basis for the argument that patents are not essential; and

---

18.In Huawei v. ZTE (EU, CJEU, 2015), the court stated that an implementer "cannot be criticized either for challenging, in parallel to the negotiations relating to the grant of licenses, the validity of those patents and/or the essential nature of those patents to the standard ··· or for reserving the right to do so in the future" and the court did not cause implementers to waive their defenses, even while indicating their willingness to take a license.

19.In Apple v. Samsung (Japan, IP high court, 2014), although the implementer Apple insisted that its product did not infringe and argued that the patent was invalid, the court found Apple to be willing to obtain a license.

20.Under U.S. law, patents can be held unenforceable if the rights holder engages in inequitable conduct before the United States Patent and Trademark Office by, for example, withholding material information with the intent to deceive (Therasense v. Becton (U.S., CAFC, 2011)).

(4) Documentation that provides the basis for the argument that patents are not enforceable.

(Reasonable Amount of Time for Response)

When reference materials provided by rights holders to implementers are not sufficient, such as not identifying the SEPs or including claim charts, it may serve to mitigate risk for the implementers to promptly request the rights holders to provide such materials.

The reasonable amount of time needed for the implementer to express its willingness to obtain a license after receiving such information from the rights holder may vary depending on various factors, such as the number of patents at issue, the complexity of the technology, the level of knowledge the implementer may have about the technology, any prior relationship, business transactions, and the state of a dispute on essentiality, validity, and infringement between the parties.

If there are relatively few patents at issue and the implementer is familiar with the technology, it may be reasonable, in some cases, for the implementer to express its willingness to obtain a license in a relatively short period of time.

On the other hand, if there are a significant number of patents at issue and the implementer is unfamiliar with the technology, several months or more may be a more reasonable time frame. For example, when a SEP-implementing component supplied by a third party is used in an end product, the end product manufacturer, if involved in the negotiations on the implementers' side, may need to obtain technical details about that component from the third-party supplier and thus may need more time to respond. If the initial substantive response requires more time, it may help to mitigate risk for the implementer to notify the rights holder and explain the specific reasons for the extra time needed so that it is not perceived as a deliberate delay (refer to II.B.1.).

(Notes on Implementers' Actions)

The following are examples of actions by an implementer that may increase the likelihood of the implementer being perceived as acting in bad faith:

(1) Not giving any reason for a very late reply or refusing to negotiate at all, even while continuing to use the infringing (or potentially infringing) technology[21];

(2) Claiming it will not start negotiation unless all grounds for essentiality and validity of the SEPs are first provided;

(3) Unreasonably delaying negotiations by, for example, persistently demanding that the rights holder provide information that cannot be disclosed due to a confidentiality

---

21.U.S. Dept of Justice and U.S. Patent and Trademark Office, Policy Statement (2013); In Apple v. Motorola (U.S., CAFC, 2014), the court stated that an injunction may be justified where an infringer unilaterally refuses a FRAND royalty or unreasonably delays negotiations to the same effect.

agreement(s) with others;

(4) Completely refusing to conclude a confidentiality agreement, while demanding that the rights holders provide claim charts, including detailed claim interpretations containing confidential information, or making repeated revisions to confidentiality agreement conditions to delay negotiations;

(5) Repeatedly making meaningless responses; or

(6) Colluding with multiple other implementers in obstinately refusing to obtain a license on the grounds that others have not obtained it.

Even when the implementer deems that the reference materials provided by the rights holder are insufficient, making no response at all may increase the likelihood of the implementer being viewed as acting in bad faith. In such a case, it may help to mitigate risk for the implementer to respond to the rights holder at least by, for example, requesting specific and necessary reference materials.

When discussions about essentiality, validity, and infringement of the SEPs are still ongoing, it may not necessarily be viewed as acting in bad faith if an implementer does not promptly express its willingness to obtain a license. On the other hand, some courts have ruled that implementers should promptly express their willingness to obtain a license while reserving their right to challenge issues of essentiality, validity, and infringement of SEPs[22][23]. Thus, from the perspective of minimizing the risk of injunction, it would be safer for an implementer to express its willingness to obtain a license at an early stage of the negotiations while reserving its right to challenge issues of SEP essentiality, validity, and infringement.

3. Step 3: Specific Offer from Rights Holder on FRAND Terms

(Overview)

If an implementer has expressed its willingness to obtain a license, the rights holder may promptly present to the implementer a written offer for a license on FRAND terms. In addition to indicating its royalty calculation method (refer to III.), the rights holder normally presents specific grounds explaining why the offer is on FRAND terms. This is done for an implementer to determine whether the presented terms are reasonable and non-discriminatory[24].

22.In St. Lawrence v. Vodafone and HTC (Germany, district court, 2016), the court stated that five months is too long to express its willingness to obtain a license after the initial warning by the rights holder, even taking into account that the implementer was a network operator and was to be allowed a certain period for consultation with the manufacturers of the challenged mobile phones. In St. Lawrence v. Deutsche Telekom and HTC (Germany, district court, 2015), the court stated that, considering that the implementer was a mobile phone manufacturer, three months was too long to express its willingness to obtain a license after the filing of an infringement lawsuit.

23.Huawei v. ZTE (EU, CJEU, 2015).

24.In Philips v. Archos (Germany, district court, 2016), since the royalty calculation method was not included in the FRAND offer, the right to seek injunctive relief was not upheld.

For portfolios containing a large number of SEPs, even in cases where a rights holder presents a royalty offer based on comparable licensing terms accepted by the market, it may still be helpful for that rights holder to provide an explanation with specific grounds sufficient for the implementer to determine whether the terms are reasonable and non-discriminatory.

Such specific grounds may include[25]:

(1) An explanation of how the rights holder calculates royalties[26] (sufficient for the implementer to objectively understand that the terms presented satisfy the FRAND obligation[27].) ; or

(2) A list of comparable licenses and their terms, if any[28], (including royalties paid to, or received from, other companies for equivalent technologies, royalties by patent pool, etc., which may or may not be disclosed depending on the terms of confidentiality agreements) (refer to II.B.3. and III.A.3.a.).

(Notes on Rights Holders' Actions)

The following are examples of actions by a rights holder that may increase the likelihood of the rights holder being perceived as acting in bad faith:

(1) Seeking an injunction against an implementer who has expressed its willingness to obtain a license on FRAND terms before offering a license on those terms, for the purpose of gaining leverage in the licensing negotiations[29][30];

(2) Sending letters warning that the rights holder will seek injunctive relief (cease-and-desist letters) to business partners of an implementer who has expressed its willingness to obtain a license on FRAND terms, despite ongoing negotiations[31];

(3) Presenting an initial offer that is clearly unreasonable given court rulings and

---

25.For example, rights holders may also be able to present prices of products or components that are used as the basis of the royalty calculation, the ownership ratio of the rights holders relative to the total number of SEPs related to the standard, and the date of expiration of patents.

26.In Sisvel v. Haier (Germany, high court, 2016), the court stated that the rights holder needed to show the factors that formed the basis of its royalty calculation.

27.In NTT DoCoMo v. HTC (Germany, district court, 2016), the court stated that the rights holder needed to make it possible for the implementer to understand that the offer satisfied FRAND terms based on objective criteria.

28.In Sisvel v. Haier (Germany, high court, 2016), the court stated that if there is a license program of the same quality and scope as the portfolio, it is necessary to make a comparison with that program.

29.In Realtek v. LSI (U.S., federal district court, 2013), the court stated that seeking injunctive relief before offering a license on FRAND terms is a breach of contractual obligations.

30.In Microsoft v. Motorola (U.S., court of appeals for the ninth circuit, 2012), the court stated that seeking injunctive relief in a related case in Germany before the decision of the U.S. court is "vexatious or oppressive".

31.In Imation v. One-Blue (Japan, district court, 2015), the court stated that it is an announcement of a falsehood and falls under unfair competition to notify a customer of the implementer who expresses its willingness to obtain a license on FRAND terms that the rights holder can seek injunctive relief.

comparable licensing terms, and sticking to that offer during the negotiation process[32]; or

(4) Not explaining how the royalty is calculated or not demonstrating that the license offer is on FRAND terms.

4. Step 4: Specific Counteroffer from Implementer on FRAND Terms

(Overview)

If an implementer disagrees with the proposed FRAND terms presented by a rights holder, the implementer may provide a FRAND counteroffer. When presenting such a counteroffer, in addition to indicating the royalty calculation method (refer to III.), the implementer normally indicates specific grounds demonstrating that its counteroffer is on FRAND terms. This is done for a rights holder to determine whether the presented terms are reasonable and nondiscriminatory.

Such specific grounds may include:

(1) An explanation of how the royalty presented by the implementer is calculated (sufficient that the rights holder can objectively understand that the terms presented satisfy the FRAND obligation); and

(2) A list of comparable licenses and their terms, if any (including royalties paid to, or received from, other companies for equivalent technologies, royalties by patent pool, etc. which may or may not be disclosed depending on the terms of confidentiality agreements) (refer to II.B.3. and III.A.3.a.)

(Reasonable Amount of Time for Response)

The reasonable time period from when an implementer receives an offer on FRAND terms from a rights holder until the implementer presents a counteroffer is determined on a case by case basis. When the technologies of the SEPs are not complicated, the implementer may present its counteroffer in a relatively short period of time. When technological complexity or other issues require a certain amount of work to prepare a response, it may be deemed reasonable for an implementer to respond in several months or more.

Factors that may determine what constitutes a reasonable amount of time to provide a counteroffer include: the number of patents at issue, the complexity of the technology, the number and type of products at issue, whether any comparable royalty rate exists,

---

32.In Microsoft v. Motorola (U.S., federal district court, 2012), the court stated that since a FRAND declaration anticipates that the parties will negotiate toward a FRAND license, it logically does not follow that the initial offers must be on FRAND terms but must comport with the implied duty of good faith and fair dealing inherent in every contract. In Unwired Planet v. Huawei (UK, high court, 2017), the court stated that offers in a negotiation that involve rates higher or lower than the FRAND rate, but do not disrupt or prejudice the negotiation, are legitimate.

and whether the parties are negotiating a worldwide license or regional license (refer to II.B.1).

(Notes on Implementers' Actions)

The following are examples of actions by an implementer that may increase the likelihood of the implementer being perceived as acting in bad faith:

(1) Not providing any counteroffer on FRAND terms after a rights holder has presented specific grounds showing that its proposed licensing terms are FRAND[33];

(2) Presenting an initial counteroffer that is clearly unreasonable given court rulings and comparable licensing terms, and sticking to that counteroffer during the negotiation process[34]; or

(3) Not explaining how a proposed royalty is calculated or not demonstrating that the counteroffer is on FRAND terms.

An implementer who does not provide a counteroffer on FRAND terms may not immediately be viewed as being in bad faith when further discussions are needed to determine the technical relationship between the subject patents and the standards as well as the validity of the patents, or when a rights holder does not provide any specific offer on FRAND terms or the basis thereof.

5. Step 5: Rejection by Rights Holder of Counteroffer/Settlement of Disputes in Courts or through ADR

(Overview)

Generally, negotiations proceed through a process of offer and counteroffer between rights holders and implementers, but if a rights holder rejects a counteroffer from the implementer and the parties fail to reach an agreement, and if one or both parties does not wish for time to go by without agreement being reached, they may be able to address their dispute in court[35].

As an alternative to litigation, the parties may agree to settle their disputes through Alternative Dispute Resolution (ADR), such as mediation or arbitration.

(Utilization of ADR)

Since it may be unrealistic for a court to determine the essentiality, validity, and

---

33. In Apple v. Motorola (U.S., CAFC, 2014), the court stated that an injunction may be justified when an implementer unilaterally refuses a FRAND royalty or unreasonably delays negotiations to the same effect. In NTT DoCoMo v. HTC (Germany, district court, 2016), the court granted injunctive relief where the implementer did not respond or make a counteroffer for 1.5 years after receiving the FRAND offer and six months after the filing of the court action.

34. See Footnote 32.

35. In Realtek v. LSI (U.S., federal district court, 2013), the court stated that if a putative implementer refuses to pay what has been determined to be a FRAND royalty, or refuses to engage in a negotiation to determine FRAND terms, an injunction could be appropriate.

infringement of dozens, or potentially even hundreds, of SEPs, a rights holder may choose several of its important patent rights to bring to court. Some argue that the greater procedural flexibility of ADR such as mediation and arbitration makes it more effective in terms of promptly settling SEP disputes over a large number of domestic and international patents.

Unless used as a tool to intentionally delay negotiations or increase cost, ADR may be a more prompt and more cost-effective approach, compared to a lawsuit[36].

In addition, parties have more flexibility in setting their own rules and procedures.

As an example, parties can agree that arbitrators will make decisions only on royalties for SEPs on FRAND terms, without considering the essentiality and validity of the SEPs[37]. In particular, an international arbitration process may be used to reach a single settlement globally as arbitral awards overseas are recognized and enforced under the New York Convention.

Some consider, however, that there are demerits to the use of ADR. For

example, ADR requires prior agreement between the disputing parties, which means that disagreements over procedures can become protracted; it is difficult to determine the validity of patent rights through ADR; and the content of ADR is undisclosed and thus lacking transparency.

Some argue that proposing or accepting the use of ADR could be considered as evidence of good faith in negotiations, while others regard it as a rather weak indicator of good or bad faith in most cases. Either way, while the refusal of ADR options may not immediately be viewed as bad faith, continuing to do so may be seen as bad faith in some cases[38].

(Security Offered by Implementers)

Under the framework presented in the CJEU decision in the case between Huawei v. ZTE, the court stated that when an alleged infringer has used SEPs before concluding any licensing agreements, from the time its counteroffer is refused, the alleged infringer is required to provide appropriate security in accordance with recognized commercial practices in Europe, for example by providing a bank guarantee or by placing the necessary amounts on deposit. It also stated that "[t]he calculation of that security must include, inter alia, the number of the past act of use of the SEP, and the alleged infringer must be able to render an account in respect of those acts of use." This is based

---

36. Although forms of ADR such as arbitration may not be quicker and more cost effective than litigation in every case, there is a view that arbitration has numerous benefits over litigation with respect to efficiency (Benefits of Arbitration for Commercial Disputes, American Bar Association).

37. There are many ways parties can structure ADR, including authorizing a neutral (or panel of neutrals) to decide certain discrete issues or make non-binding recommendations as to those issues.

38. In Huawei v. Samsung (China, intermediate court, 2018).

on the idea that it would be contradictory and therefore unfair for the implementer to assert its willingness to pay the license fee but actually fail to do so even while using the product.

Although providing such security may be a factor in considering good faith, an implementer's failure to offer security may not necessarily increase the likelihood of being viewed as bad faith in regions outside Europe, such as Japan and the United States. There is a view, however, that where an implementer lacks the financial capability to meet its financial obligations under a license ultimately to be concluded, the implementer could be viewed as acting in bad faith for not providing appropriate security.

There is also a view that the provision of security gives both parties the incentive to negotiate in good faith.

(Exercise of Right to Seek Injunction)

Around the world, there has been an accumulation of legal precedents concerning SEP-related injunctions. Most courts have imposed limitations on the exercise of the right to seek an injunction against implementers who have responded in good faith, and have determined that it would be appropriate for a rights holder to be allowed to exercise its right to seek an injunction when implementers have responded in bad faith during the negotiation process.

Nonetheless, grounds for restricting the rights of SEP owners to seek injunctions vary by country. For example, there have been cases in which the exercise of the right to seek an injunction was restricted based on, in the United States, the requirements for seeking injunction, as detailed in the decision by the Supreme Court in the eBay case and the contractual effects of FRAND declarations to SSOs on third parties[39]; in the U.K., the contractual effects of FRAND declarations to SSOs on third parties[40]; in Europe, a violation of the Competition Law by the rights holder's abuse of its dominant position[41];

---

39. In the United States, in general, an injunction (35 U.S.C. 283) takes into account the four requirements identified in eBay v. MercExchange (U.S., Supreme Court, 2006). A plaintiff must demonstrate: (1) that it has suffered an irreparable injury; (2) that remedies available at law, such as monetary damages, are inadequate to compensate for that injury; (3) that, considering the balance of hardships between the plaintiff and defendant, a remedy in equity is warranted; and (4) that the public interest would not be disserved by a permanent injunction. Regarding SEPs, in both Microsoft v. Motorola (U.S., federal district court, 2013) and Apple v. Motorola (U.S., CAFC, 2014), the court regarded the FRAND commitments to the SSO as a contract between the rights holder and the SSO for a third-party beneficiary, and did not grant injunctive relief because the rights holder did not satisfy one of the factors in eBay (U.S., Supreme Court, 2006), namely "that it has suffered an irreparable injury," because the contract between the two parties enabled the rights holder to obtain relief via the royalty paid by the implementer. In Apple v. Motorola, parties' attitudes toward negotiations are also considered as a factor.

40. In Unwired Planet v. Huawei (U.K., high court, 2017), the court stated that the contractual effect of the FRAND declaration to an SSO will extend to third parties.

41. In Huawei v. ZTE (EU, CJEU, 2015), the court identified the steps that the rights holder must take before seeking injunctive relief, such as alerting the implementer or presenting a specific, written offer for a license on FRAND terms. The court held that if the implementer improperly delays after these steps are taken by the rights holder, an injunction will not violate competition law and seeking injunctive relief will be justified.

and in Japan, the rights holder's abuse of patent rights[42].

Also, competition authorities in Japan and Europe suggest that demanding an injunction against an entity that is willing to obtain a license on FRAND terms may be a violation of competition law[43]. The competition authority in the United States does not agree that this conduct comprises the basis for a competition violation[44].

B. Efficiency

To conduct licensing negotiations smoothly, it is also important to consider efficiency along with good faith. The following sections address key points that should be considered for the efficient conduct of FRAND-based negotiations.

[Factors for Efficient Negotiation]
1. Notification of a Timeframe
2. Parties to Negotiation in Supply Chain
3. Protecting Confidential Information
4. Choice of Patents subject to Negotiation
5. Geographic Scope of License Agreement
6. Patent Pool Licensing
7. Greater Transparency of SEPs

1. Notification of a Timeframe

For negotiations to proceed smoothly, it is desirable for the parties to notify
each other of the overall expected timeframe as well as the timeframe required for each of the stages identified in II.A above.

The negotiation timeframe may vary widely. Factors that may be considered in setting reasonable expectations for a timeframe may include, but are not limited to: the number of patents at issue, the complexity of the technology, the number of different products and types/nature of the products at issue, matters pending in the courts or patent offices that relate to issues underlying the negotiation (e.g., essentiality and validity), and the number of licenses the patent owner has already granted for the SEPs.

42.In Japan, there is no provision that limits an injunction in general, but regarding SEPs, in Apple v. Samsung (Japan, IP high court, 2014), seeking injunctive relief against a person who is willing to obtain a license was deemed to be an abuse of rights.

43.See, for example, Motorola v. Apple (EU, EC, 2014); Samsung v. Apple (EU, EC, 2014); "Guidelines for the Use of Intellectual Property under the Antimonopoly Act" (The Japan Fair Trade Commission, 2016).

44.Makan Delrahim, Assistant Attorney General, Antitrust Division, U.S. Department of Justice (DOJ), stated as a view of the DOJ that "it is just as important to recognize that a violation by a patent holder of an SSO rule that restricts a patent-holder's right to seek injunctive relief should be appropriately the subject of a contract or fraud action, and rarely if ever should be an antitrust violation."

In the case that an implementer seeks to secure a relatively long negotiation timeframe, there is a view that the specific grounds need to be explained to the rights holder to gain their understanding.

Naturally, as discussions proceed, there may be events that require the timeframe to be changed. Nonetheless, discussing and clarifying the expected timeframe early on can enable both parties develop a shared sense of the likely negotiation timeframe[45].

In particular, with product lifecycles becoming shorter, there is some concern that prolonged negotiations could prevent the timely recovery of the investment that would allow for investment in next-generation technologies. Some argue that protracted negotiations may also lead to engineers and other resources that should have been channeled into R&D instead being used for negotiations, creating a major burden.

While some consider that notifying the estimated length of time for licensing negotiations may increase the likelihood of that party being perceived as acting in good faith, others suggest that not doing so will not necessarily be perceived as bad faith.

2. Parties to Negotiation in Supply Chain

(Overview)

With the spread of IoT, the use of standards has become more common. One issue often arising during negotiations is which entities in the manufacturing supply chain should be parties to licensing negotiations (e.g., component suppliers versus end-product manufacturers). There may not be a problem in selecting the parties to a negotiation as long as the parties can agree based on industry practices. Problems may arise, however, if, for example, a component installed in the end product implements a SEP.

While the level of the main parties to negotiations should be determined on a case by case basis, in the interests of, for example, making license management easier, rights holders generally tend to want to conclude license agreements with the end-product manufacturer[46].46 On the other hand, the end-product manufacturer tends to want the supplier that has the most technical knowledge on the subject component to be the party involved in negotiating and concluding the licensing agreement. This tendency is especially evident in industries where the general practice is for the supplier to accept a patent indemnification agreement that puts the burden of licensing fees on the

---

45.While the overall negotiation timeframe will vary by case, some suggest as a rough reference to what prompt completion might look like that complex cross licenses with vast portfolios might complete in 12 months, one-way licenses with fewer SEP families at stake in 9- 12 months, and simple one-way licenses with a few patents in 6-9 months. Others, however, do not like the idea of any numerical benchmark for negotiation timeframes.

46.While some argue that the reason that rights holders want to negotiate with end-product manufacturers is that they hope they will be able to gain more royalties that way, just as licensing rates change according to the basis of calculation (refer to III.A.2.), licensing rates too change according to where the main parties to the negotiation stand in the supply chain (lower for endproduct manufacturers and higher for component suppliers), leading some parties to suggest that negotiating with end-product manufacturers does not necessarily produce more royalties.

supplier. (Implementer Who Will be the Party to Licensing Negotiations) In general, the rights holder is in the position to decide with which party in the supply chain it signs an agreement, e.g., end-product manufacturer, component manufacturer, or sub-component manufacturer.

Meanwhile, there is some debate globally on whether FRAND-encumbered SEPs should be licensed to anyone who desires to obtain such a license[47][48].

There are some end-product manufacturers that consider it discriminatory and contrary to FRAND commitments if the rights holder refuses to negotiate with the supplier manufacturing the component when it requests to be the party to the licensing negotiations. On the other hand, some consider it inappropriate for the endproduct manufacturer to refuse all negotiations when the rights holder requests it to be the party to the licensing negotiations.

In addition, some argue that if the essential part of the patented invention is used only in the components provided by the supplier, it is appropriate for the supplier to be the party to the licensing negotiations. Others argue that if the essential part of the patented invention contributes to the end product, it is appropriate for the end-product manufacturer to be the party in licensing negotiations.

In any case, since there is a risk that injunctive relief against infringement may be granted against entities regardless of whether they are suppliers or end-product manufacturers if no entity in the supply chain obtains the license, all supply chain entities need to be aware of the status of conclusion of licensing agreements.

(Arguments from the Standpoint of Number of Players)

Some argue that having the end-product manufacturer involved in negotiations is most efficient, in that the licensing negotiations can then cover all the components contained in a product and consequently minimize the number of necessary negotiations as well as reduce negotiation costs, while also avoiding issues such as discrepancies in the licensing terms between suppliers[49].

On the other hand, others suggest that there may also be cases in which including suppliers in the negotiations is more efficient, such as when a small number of suppliers are supplying components to a large number of end-product manufacturers, and

---

47.The idea that rights holders must license all entities wishing to obtain licenses regardless of the level in the supply chain is commonly referred as "license to all." On the other hand, the idea that the FRAND declaration is not a requirement for licensing to all parties using standard technology, but is rather a mechanism to ensure that those who want to use standard technology can access that technology is commonly referred as "access for all."

48.In 2015, the Institute of Electrical and Electronics Engineers (IEEE) amended its patent policy to state that rights holders should be willing to make licenses available to anyone who requests a license. Objections to this amendment have been made by rights holders (IEEE-SA Standards Board Bylaws (2015)).

49.One view is that where SEPs are not limited to a component (i.e., a portfolio of SEPs covering more than just one component), it may be unnecessarily complicating to include component suppliers in negotiations because that will result in splitting up or sub-categorizing the portfolio.

the rights holders can minimize the number of negotiations by conducting licensing negotiations with such suppliers.

(Arguments from the Standpoint of Exhaustion and Double Earnings)
It is generally considered that when a product that is protected by a patent is placed legitimately on the market by a rights holder or a licensed implementer, the patent is exhausted, so the rights holder may not exercise its rights against someone who has purchased the product[50].In this connection, if a rights holder concludes licensing agreements with multiple suppliers within a single supply chain, some are concerned that it may become unclear which right has been exhausted, and could more readily lead to the issue of double earnings by the rights holder or underpayment to the rights holder. Others argue that such issues may be avoided by conducting licensing negotiations with the end-product manufacturer.

Another view, however, is that end-product manufacturers face difficulties in ascertaining the status of licensing agreements concluded upstream and in identifying a double-earnings issue, and therefore that the involvement in negotiations of those parties manufacturing components included in the technical scope of patent rights is valuable in terms of avoiding the double-earnings issue.

(Arguments from the Standpoint of Technical Knowledge)
Some argue that where an end-product manufacturer without detailed knowledge of the technologies involved is the main party to the negotiation, they will need to coordinate with all their suppliers throughout the negotiation process, which may lengthen the process and also push up the cost. Accordingly, they argue that it may be more efficient for those suppliers of technologies that fall within the scope of the patent claims, who consequently have the necessary technical knowledge, to be party to licensing negotiations.

Conversely, there is also a suggestion from the perspective of rights holders wishing to negotiate with end-product manufacturers that it is possible to acquire information on the technical content from the suppliers without involving them in the negotiations.

(Sharing the Burden of Licensing Fees)

50.In the United States, when a component manufacturer has a patent license and an end product incorporating the licensed component is sold, it may not be possible to obtain a royalty from the end-product manufacturer because the patent is exhausted by the first sale of the component (Quanta v. LG (U.S., Supreme Court, 2008)). That is, a sold component may exhaust patents to a larger product when the component "substantially embod[ies] the essential features of the patent when the only reasonable and intended use [of the component] is to practice the patent [in the larger product]." On the other hand, in Apple v. Samsung (Japan, IP high court, 2014), the court stated that when rights holders sell components used only for the manufacture of a patented product, the patent is exhausted while when a third party does not even have an implied license and is manufacturing the end-product using that component, the patent is not exhausted.

When the rights holder requests payment of licensing fees after the product is sold, how this payment burden should be distributed within the supply chain sometimes becomes an issue. In particular, in the ICT industry, this issue tends to occur because entities commonly start licensing negotiations after the service is launched.

There are certain industries in which a patent indemnification agreement may be concluded whereby the supplier shoulders the payment of licensing fees. In such situations, even when the license fee negotiated by the end-product manufacturer as the party is excessive and disproportionate to the price of the component, the supplier may be requested to bear the burden[51].

To avoid such a situation, some patent indemnification agreements exempt SEPs. Some argue that, in order to avoid an excessive burden on suppliers, licensing fees should be apportioned out across the supply chain according to the essential parts of the invention within the scope of the patent claim.

Others suggest that it may be reasonable to incorporate in a patent indemnification agreement a provision to exempt the supplier from responsibility to pay the licensing fee if the supplier was not given the chance to be involved in the licensing negotiations. Some have also suggested that it might be reasonable to include a provision that exempts suppliers from the responsibility to pay more than an amount corresponding to the price of the component. Another opinion is that if suppliers are required to shoulder licensing fees, the price for their components should reflect the technical value of the SEP.

3. Protecting Confidential Information

(Overview)

A confidentiality agreement (non-disclosure agreement) ensures that information that is sensitive from a business or technical perspective and that is disclosed during negotiations is not disclosed in turn to a third party. By concluding a confidentiality agreement, the parties may find it easier to disclose sensitive information, thus leading to a more efficient licensing negotiation.

On the other hand, a party should take care in the wording of a confidentiality agreement to avoid the risk of being prevented from presenting information later in court as proof of good faith negotiations.

(Confidential Information of the Implementers)

Potentially confidential implementer information might include businessrelated information (e.g. market forecasts and sales information, etc.), and technical information

---

51.There has been a ruling that where suppliers party to patent indemnification agreements do not meet their obligation to provide end-product manufacturers with the necessary documents, etc., they should shoulder part of the licensing fee paid by the end-product manufacturer to the rights holder (Softbank v. Kanematsu (Japan, IP high court, 2015)).

about the implementer's products that is not publicly available.

If the rights holder exercises SEPs over products or methods of manufacture not open to the public, an implementer may want to consider whether to disclose proprietary technical information (such as blueprints of semiconductors or software source code) in order to counter effectively the specific grounds for infringement presented by the rights holder.

By contrast, if the allegedly infringing product which is the subject of the negotiations is one which the rights holder can obtain to assess whether there is an infringement of its patents, such as a general-purpose mechanical invention, it may be apparent from inspection of the product whether it practices the patent(s), and the disclosure of confidential technical information by the implementer may not be required.

When the subjects of discussion are centered on the correspondence between patent claims and the standard documents, there may be cases where the implementer does not need to disclose confidential technical information regarding the product.

(Confidential Information of Rights Holders)

Potentially confidential rights holder information might include an explanation of claim terminology and the corresponding sections in the standard documents (refer to II.A.1.), and the terms of comparable licenses, such as the rate or the amount used to explain and support a FRAND offer.

(Provisions for a Confidentiality Agreement)

When concluding a confidentiality agreement, the following are examples of provisions that may be discussed depending on the circumstances of each negotiation:

(1) Which information needs to be kept confidential

(2) Who will receive confidential information

(3) How will confidential information be marked

(4) Whether orally communicated information will be covered

(5) The duration of the agreement

(6) Whether information can later be used in litigation as a defense

(7) The duration of the confidentiality obligation

(8) Information exempted from confidentiality (information within the public domain and legitimately acquired information, etc.)

(Maintaining Confidentiality of the Process, Content, and Result of the Licensing Negotiations)

The parties may also consider setting forth confidentiality provisions applicable to the process, content, and result of the licensing negotiations. On the one hand, facts such as what kind of information has been disclosed at what point in a series of negotiations is often important in reading other parties' thinking on and approach to business and to patents, and parties often want complete confidentiality, to the extent that even the existence of a resulting license agreement is confidential, so as to ensure against, for example the deliberate choice of only certain parts of the negotiation proceedings for disclosure.

On the other hand, often the existence and the content of the licensing agreement are not treated as confidential so that the agreement may be assessed as a "comparable license" in the future. The parties may want to consider, in view of the above, for example, whether all terms and the existence of an agreement will be confidential, whether only its monetary terms will be confidential, or whether only sales volume information (e.g., past sales) will be confidential, etc.

4. Choice of Patents Subject to Negotiation

Whether licensing negotiations are conducted on a portfolio basis or by patent is determined by the parties on a case by case basis. SEP licensing negotiations are often conducted as portfolio negotiations from the standpoint of a comprehensive settlement. When rights holders possess a large number of SEPs, however, the parties may discuss limiting the subject of the negotiation to "representative" patents so as to streamline the negotiation process. When doing so, there is a view that it may be desirable for the parties to explain the reason for selecting the patents as representative.

As an example, in a case involving several hundred SEPs, the parties may hold discussions on just those patents deemed the most valuable (generally 30 at most)[52], or select random samples to efficiently assess the total value. They might also independently categorize the patents into tiers, analyze the top few from each tier to get an idea of the topology of the overall portfolio's quality, and get together to compare results. In such cases, one view is that concluding all licensing agreements, including those SEPs that were not the subject of discussion, as a single package is an efficient approach in terms of administration.

The parties may also discuss whether the negotiations will include non-SEPs in addition to SEPs[53]. While it is up to the parties to choose which particular patents will be included, it may, for example, be efficient to include in the negotiation a commercially essential patent (a patent for which there exists a technical alternative but which is

---

52. In Sisvel v. Haier (Germany, high court, 2016), the court asked the rights holder to present a "proud list" of 10-15 patents from a portfolio of over 400 patents and to explain the reason for choosing them.

53. It should be kept in mind that licensing negotiations where rights holders seek to cover non-SEPs in addition to SEPs do not conflict with the "tying" of competition law, provided that rights holders do not use their market power to coerce payment for non-SEPs. There is a view that portfolio licensing can be efficient under competition law principles and that such licensing efficiencies have the potential to outweigh competition concerns associated with tying. (U.S. Dep't of Justice and Federal Trade Commission, Antitrust Guidelines (2017)).

practically inescapable due to cost/performance issues)[54]or non-SEPs. There are also cases of licensing through frameworks whereby implementers can choose which SEPs they wish to license[55].

5. Geographic Scope of Licensing Agreement

With regard to the geographic scope of a license, parties generally consider whether a license will be limited to particular regions or globally applicable. When setting the geographic scope, the parties may want to consider on a case by case basis whether the implementer is producing or selling products in multiple regions throughout the world, as well as how many patents the rights holder holds and the strength thereof, in those jurisdictions[56].

Some argue that, given the international distribution of ICT and other standardized technologies, it would be more efficient to address SEPs in all countries and regions in which an implementer may produce and/or sell its products in future in addition to those countries and regions where it currently does so[57]. There is also a view that global licensing agreements allow easier and more efficient license management, as, for example, they do not require agreements to be amended if the implementer expands its business geographically. Others argue that an implementer may well conclude a licensing agreement covering only those countries or regions where it is operating or has a concrete plan to operate.

Also, there are some cases of global licenses granted on different licensing terms for different regions[58].

If the implementer is producing and/or selling its product in multiple regions, there is a view that where the implementer requests a licensing agreement for patent rights only in such specific countries/regions with consideration to the specific circumstances of the patents in each, care should be taken to prevent this from turning into a delaying tactic

---

54.Certain SSOs explicitly rule out the concept of commercial essentiality in their IPR policies, defining essentiality solely on a technical basis (patents covering a technology must a technical or engineering matter).

55.For example, in some patent pools, SEPs are divided into basic functions and options, and the implementer can choose the scope of the SEP which they wish to license.

56.There are various discussions about courts setting licensing terms globally. In Unwired Planet v. Huawei (U.K., high court, 2017), although Huawei as the implementer refused to allow the court to set global licensing terms, the court set the licensing terms globally. Meanwhile, in TCL v. Ericsson (U.S., federal district court, 2017), the court set the licensing terms globally, because of the fact that the TCL, the implementer, had already agreed to allow the court to set global licensing terms.

57.In Unwired Planet v. Huawei (U.K., high court, 2017), the court found it reasonable to address SEPs in all countries and regions in which the implementers currently produce and/or sell and/or may do so in future.

58.In Unwired Planet v. Huawei (UK, high court, 2017), the court found that licenses granted on FRAND terms are global, while taking regional differences into consideration, it showed different royalty rates among different markets. In TCL v. Ericsson (U.S., federal district court, 2017), the court divided regions into the United States, Europe, and the rest of the world and set the royalty rates globally. It should be noted that certain entities disagree with the authority of a court to set license terms outside of its jurisdiction when one of the parties questions whether it is within the court's authority to set such terms.

in the negotiations.

6. Patent Pool Licensing

In patent pools, wide participation by rights holders and implementers may produce licensing terms that balance the interests of both, which may boost the efficiency of licensing negotiations compared to individual bilateral negotiations amongst multiple parties[59].

Where a rights holder participates in a patent pool, the general practice is for that rights holder to approach licensing negotiations with implementers through the body managing the patent pool.

Additionally, patent rights that are registered in a pool are normally checked to some extent for essentiality by a third party. Although this does not necessarily guarantee essentiality, it is expected that it may lead to greater SEP transparency.

On the other hand, there are some cases where standard-related licensing issues cannot be resolved in one patent pool, such as where there are rights holders granting licenses individually, where there are multiple patent pools, or where there are companies holding other patents such as commercially essential patents.

Some point out that patent pools do not necessarily improve efficiency if rights holders who grant licenses individually participate in the patent pool, as this may cause double royalty earnings on the part of such rights holders. Because of this, some patent pools establish mechanisms to prevent double royalty earnings[60].

Implementers aiming to resolve disputes through cross licensing must bear in mind that this will not be possible with bodies managing patent pools that are not implementing the invention. There is also a view that patent pool participation does not rule out cross licensing, and that an implementer can simply pay the royalties of those pool members with which it does not have a cross licensing agreement.

7. Greater Transparency of SEPs

Enhancing transparency in regard to the essentiality and validity of SEPs leads to more efficient licensing negotiations. The European Communication expects SSOs to promote the development of databases with information on SEPs[61]. It also expects rights holders to provide information on SEPs to SSOs, so the SSOs can then update their information. With SSOs building up databases and widely providing information on SEPs, it will become easier for rights holders to obtain the necessary documents when presenting

---

59. Refer to III.A.3.a.(c) on the licensing terms for pooled patents.

60. For example, in the case that an implementer already has a licensing agreement with a rights holder, there are agreements whereby the royalty amount that is already agreed is subtracted from the royalty amount set for the pool.

61. The European Communication urges SSOs to improve the quality of their SEP database in order to enhance transparency on SEPs and refers to launching a pilot project on the standard essentiality of SEPs.

offers for licensing negotiations or FRAND licensing terms. It will also become easier for implementers to obtain information on SEPs related to relevant standards.

On the other hand, there is also a view that rights holders may need to be compensated for the cost of boosting transparency and the possibility of their own patents being deemed inessential or invalid that is inherent in enhancing SSO databases, so as not to reduce the motivation to participate in standardization.

III. Royalty Calculation Methods

As mentioned earlier, there are two aspects of FRAND: (i) the negotiation process itself and (ii) the terms of a license. This chapter will address the second aspect of FRAND. FRAND licensing terms include not only royalties but also non-monetary aspects such as cross-licensing, but because there are no established criteria for reasonable and non-discriminatory royalties in SEP licensing negotiations, the parties often disagree on the appropriate FRAND terms.

Therefore, this chapter will address royalty calculation methods in detail, based on standard practices and the framework indicated by past court rulings. It should be noted, however, that this Guide only identifies issues that may be considered in relation to calculation methods and does not direct any particular way for parties to arrive at a specific royalty rate or amount. Royalty rate calculation methods should be determined flexibly by the parties on a case by case basis, and the calculation methods outlined in this chapter may not necessarily be used.

A. Reasonable Royalties

1. Basic Approach

Royalties reflect the value that the patent has contributed to the product and therefore is obtained by:

(1) Royalty base (Calculation base) x (2) Royalty ratio (Rate)

This approach may also be applied to the calculation of SEP royalties. There has been intense discussion, however, on issues such as how to handle the value added after a technology has been incorporated into a standard, how to identify the calculation base, and how to calculate the royalty rate. These issues are discussed further below[62].

(Value Added after Incorporation into a Standard)

62.For example, U.S. courts often apply the fifteen Georgia-Pacific factors (referred to as "GPF") for calculating the royalty. With FRAND-encumbered SEPs, modified GPFs have been adopted. (Microsoft v. Motorola (U.S., federal district court, 2013))

There is a view that SEP royalties should reflect only the value of the patented technology before the standard is widely adopted in the market (generally called "ex ante"). This is based on the idea that, when a technology is being considered to form part of a standard, it is selected from multiple technological options, while once it is incorporated into the standard, it is used only out of necessity to adhere to the standard[63]. Based on this premise, there are cases where the royalty is assessed at a point in time before the standard is widely used and set promptly after the standard is announced, then kept at that level regardless of the success or failure in the markets of the products implementing the SEPs.

On the other hand, there is a view that the "ex ante" approach is not practical in calculating the damages for infringement of patent rights because the amount of damages should incorporate the value of the patented invention at the time of implementation, and a part of such value is created by the technology successfully becoming the standard. Furthermore, there is also a view that it is inappropriate to adopt the "ex ante" approach because it would lead to the profit from standardization being distributed only to implementers and not to rights holders[64].

2. Royalty Base (Calculation Base)

(Identification of the Problem)

As for the calculation base, debate has centered on whether the smallest salable patent practicing unit ("SSPPU")[65]or the entire market value ("EMV")[66]should be adopted[67]. The SSPPU approach is based on the premise that if a SEP technology is used only in the component that is the SSPPU, the price of that component to which the SEP is considered to contribute will then be the calculation base. Meanwhile, the EMV is an approach taken when the SEP technology is considered to contribute to the function of the whole end product and to drive demand for the product, and the price of the whole end product will be the calculation base.

63.See Ericsson v. D-Link (U.S., CAFC, 2014).

64.In Unwired Planet v. Huawei (UK, high court, 2017), the court stated that the rights holder could appropriate some of the value that is associated with the inclusion of the technology into the standard and the value of the products using the standards.

65.In In re Innovatio (U.S., federal district court, 2013), the court stated that the top-down approach starts with the average price of a Wi-Fi chip. In Virnetx v. Cisco (U.S., CAFC, 2014) the court stated that "[w]here the smallest salable unit is, in fact, a multi-component product containing several non-infringing features with no relation to the patented feature···, the patentee must do more to estimate what portion of the value of that product is attributable to the patented technology."

66.In CSIRO v. Cisco (U.S., CAFC, 2015), the court stated that if a party can prove that the patented invention drives demand for the accused end product, it can rely on the end-product's entire market value as the royalty base.

67.In LaserDynamics v. Quanta (U.S., CAFC, 2012), the court stated that it is generally required that royalties be based on the SSPPU approach, citing the concept of "the smallest salable infringing unit" in Cornell University v. Hewlett-Packard (U.S., federal district court, 2009), but stated that if it can be shown that the patented feature drives the demand for an entire multicomponent product, the entire product could be used as the royalty base, and rights holders may be awarded damages as a percentage of revenues or profits attributable to the entire product.

While these are approaches devised by courts in calculating damages equivalent to a reasonable implementing fee in patent infringement cases, they could also be used in actual licensing negotiations as a reference in determining reasonable royalties.

There are many cases in which the rights holder has insisted on the adoption of the EMV approach based on its view that the SEP technology contributes to the function of the entire end product and drives product demand. Likewise, there are many cases in which the end-product manufacturer has insisted on adoption of the SSPPU approach based on its view that the contributions of the SEP technology are confined to just a portion or component of the overall end product.

In the days when debate focused on cellular phones, where communication technology was central to functionality, many parties supported the use of EMV.

The emergence of products such as smart phones and self-driving cars for which communications technology accounts only for a part of the product's functions, however, has raised debate over the use of SSPPU or EMV.

(Approach to the Calculation Base)

A feature shared by both approaches (SSPPU and EMV) is the attempt to identify the calculation base according to where the contribution of the essential part of the SEP lies[68].

In addition, the SSPPU and the EMV methodologies are not the only possibilities for considering a royalty base. The point is that a suitable calculation base for each individual case should be considered.

For example, some argue that when the essential part of the SEP technology supports the operation of functions of a device larger than a chip and contributes to the functions of the device beyond the chip itself, using the price of the chip as the SSPPU may not reflect the real value provided by the SEP technology.

On the other hand, other suggest that when the contribution of the essential part of the SEP technology is confined to the chip itself and the chip is independent and has an objective market value, the price of the chip may be deemed appropriate as the calculation base.

Even when the SEP technology goes beyond a particular chip, there is a view that the SSPPU is an effective starting point for discussion in accumulatively and elaborately analyzing the product portions to which the SEP technology contributes.

This view emphasizes that the basis of the calculation should not exceed the scope of the contribution of the essential part of the SEP technology for which a license is being sought.

68.In Ericsson v. D-Link (U.S., CAFC, 2014), the court stated that the ultimate reasonable royalty award must be based on the incremental value that the patented invention adds to the end product.

Contrarily, there is an approach using the EMV as the starting point of discussion and determining the calculation base by multiplying the end product by the ratio of the contribution to the end product of all the SEPs that cover the technical standard[69].

There is a view that the EMV approach may lead to a high calculation base with a fixed rate, resulting in a high royalty. Conversely, there is another view that the SSPPU approach may reduce the base with a fixed rate, resulting in a low royalty.

Some argue, however, that when the calculation base is small, the rate will be high, while a large calculation base causes the rate to be low, selecting the calculation base not directly relevant to the resulting royalty amount in theory.

3. Royalty Rate

(Approaches to Rate Determination)

Of the many different approaches to determining an appropriate royalty rate, two frequently identified in court decisions are (i) determining the share of contribution of a particular SEP, by referencing, for example, existing comparable licenses (bottom-up approach); and (ii) calculating the share in the calculation base of the contribution of all SEPs for a given standard and then allotting a share to individual SEPs (top-down approach).

These two approaches are not contradictory. Both approaches may be combined to calculate the rate so as to ensure a more reliable rate through comparison of the results[70]. When there is an existing comparable license, some argue for referring to it[71], whereas others argue for taking the top-down approach that first considers the contribution of all SEPs even in that situation.

a. Bottom-Up Approach

Examples of comparable licenses include those of patents owned by the same rights holder and patents owned by others essential to the same standard or a similar standard. The following are examples of factors that have been considered in court cases and practice in determining whether a license is comparable:

(1) Whether the license is for the same or similar patents,

---

69. In Apple v. Samsung (Japan, IP high court, 2014), because the design, use interface, camera, audio function, etc. contribute to the product in addition to the wireless communication function, the court stated that the basis of the calculation should be multiplied by the rate that it is deemed was contributing to the product by complying with the standard (contribution rate).

70. In Unwired Planet v. Huawei case (UK, high court, 2017), while adopting a bottom-up approach, the court double-checked whether royalty stacking has occurred with a top-down approach. On the other hand, in TCL v. Ericsson case (U.S., federal district court, 2017).), while adopting a top-down approach, the court double-checked with a bottom-up approach.

71. In Laser Dynamics v. Quanta (U.S., CAFC 2012), the court stated that actual licenses for the patented technology are highly probative as to what constitutes a reasonable royalty for those patent rights, because such actual licenses most clearly reflect the economic value of the patented technology in the marketplace.

(2) Whether the license covers unrelated technology or different products[72],

(3) Whether the license has a similar fee structure (e.g., lump-sum or running royalty)

(4) Whether the nature of the license is the same in terms of exclusivity[73]

(5) Whether the license applies to similar territories (e.g., a regional or global license)

(6) Whether the terms of the license are widely accepted

(7) Whether the license has been achieved through a court settlement or through normal negotiations

(8) How recent the license is, and

(9) Whether the licensee has a sufficient negotiating strength to enable balanced negotiations.

(a) Comparable Licenses Held by the Same Patent Holder

In practice, it is often difficult to identify existing licenses that are identical or sufficiently similar to a potential license under discussion. On the one hand, when existing licensing agreements were concluded under circumstances that differ from the parties' present circumstances, the existing licenses may generally be referenced when the parties determine the royalty rate if they can account for the differences, but the effectiveness of such references may vary depending on the level of difference[74][75].

When there are great differences between the circumstances of an existing license and present circumstances and it is difficult to reasonably account for such differences, it may then be difficult to consider the existing license as being comparable and it will have less value in determining an appropriate royalty rate[76].

(b) Comparable Licenses Held by Third Parties

In referring to the existing licensing terms of third parties who hold SEPs for the same standard, it may be possible to calculate an appropriate rate by comparing the number of SEPs owned by the rights holder to those held by the third party and multiplying the ratio obtained.

In this case, the rate may be adjusted taking into account the value of the specific SEPs. It should also be noted that some third parties inflate the number of SEPs through

---

72. In ResQNet v. Lansa (U.S., CAFC, 2010), the court stated that the trial court should not rely on unrelated licenses to increase the reasonable royalty rate above rates more clearly linked to the economic demand for the claimed technology.

73. In Lucent v. Gateway (U.S., CAFC, 2009), the court stated that GPF3 (exclusive or nonexclusive) is applicable as a consideration factor.

74. In Ericsson v. D-Link (U.S., CAFC, 2014), the court stated that allegedly comparable licenses may cover more patents than are at issue in the action, include cross-licensing terms, cover foreign intellectual property rights, or, as here, be calculated as some percentage of the value of a multi-component product.

75. In Virnetx v. Cisco (U.S., CAFC, 2014), the court stated that the "degree of comparability" of the license agreements is applicable as a consideration factor.

76. In Laser Dynamics v. Quanta (U.S., CAFC 2012), the court stated that the propriety of using prior settlement agreements to prove the amount of a reasonable royalty is questionable. On the other hand, there are some arguments that licenses in litigation could also be referred to as comparable licenses.

divisional patent applications.

Some view the limited availability of comparable licenses held by third parties and the difficulty of evaluating other parties' portfolios as standing in the way of making comparisons of licensing terms.

(c) Patent Pools

As a reference in determining a FRAND rate, parties may compare the rate charged by a patent pool for the same standard. If the degree of contribution to the standard of SEPs owned by the rights holder is higher than that to the patents in the patent pool, the rate for the SEPs may be higher than that for the patent pool.

Meanwhile, if the degree of contribution to the standard of SEPs owned by the rights holders is lower than that to the patents in the patent pool, the rate for the SEPs may be lower than that for the patent pool.

It may also be necessary to note that, a relatively low royalty is set as a result of taking into account the fact that negotiations, contracts, and the management of royalties are streamlined in many patent pools[77], while some pools choose to set a relatively high royalty by including non-essential patents.

The licensing terms of a patent pool are not always comparable. The coverage rate and licensing record of the patent pool may be considered to assess whether there is comparability[78].

There may also be cases where the patent pool situation differs from that of licenses negotiated bilaterally because the rate is set by multiple rights holders. It should also be noted that some rights holders are inflating SEP numbers through divisional patent applications.

b. Top-Down Approach

(Overview)

Determining an appropriate rate by calculating the ratio of the contribution of all the SEPs for the standard in the calculation base is generally known as the topdown approach. In this approach, the aggregate royalty rate is calculated as the extent of the contribution of all SEPs to the standard (total royalty rate for all SEPs that cover the

---

77.In Microsoft v. Motorola (U.S., federal district court, 2013), the court concluded that the royalty was triple the pool royalty.

78.In Microsoft v. Motorola (U.S., federal district court, 2013), the court stated that the problem with using patent pools as the de facto RAND royalty rate is that the patent-counting royalty allocation structure of pools does not consider the importance of a particular SEP to the standard or to the implementer's products as the court's hypothetical negotiation requires.

standard), then allotted to individual SEPs[79].

(Avoiding Royalty Stacking)

When many rights holders individually demand royalties, there may be cases in which each royalty "stacks up," making the cost for practicing the standard excessively high. This is called royalty stacking, and is an issue that may occur when there are many rights holders that hold SEPs for the same standard.

As the extent of the contribution of all SEPs to the standards defines the total rate, there is a view that the top-down approach is effective in avoiding such royalty stacking. From this standpoint, when the bottom-up approach is used, it may be beneficial to check for royal stacking by also making a calculation using the topdown approach.

While some parties believe that royalty stacking is occurring in practice, others suggest that there is no concrete proof of this.

4. Other Factors to Consider in Determining Rates

In addition to the calculation base and the rate described above, other factors may also be considered in practice, as identified below.

a. Number of Licensees that Agreed to the Royalty Rate

The more licensees have agreed to a particular rate, the easier it may be to show that it is an established royalty rate and FRAND. Therefore, the number of existing licensees may be taken into consideration.

On the other hand, some point out that the number of licensees may not be relevant in the initial phase of licensing activities.

b. Scope of License[80]

In determining the appropriate royalty, the parties may also consider whether there is a restriction on where or to whom to sell the products.

c. Essentiality/Validity/Infringement of Patent

If a patent turns out to be inessential to a standard or invalid, or if there is no infringement, there is normally no need to obtain a license for the patent in order to implement the standard. An implementer, however, may make a business judgement to sign licensing agreements, even if it not convinced of essentiality, validity,

---

79.In Apple v. Samsung (Japan, IP high court, 2014), the court adopted a top-down approach and set the aggregate royalty rate at 5% for 3G based on the claims of the parties. In addition, in TCL v. Ericsson (U.S., federal district court, 2017), the court set the aggregate royalty at 5% for 2G/3G and at 6% or 10% for 4G.

80.Corresponding to GPF3.

or infringement, because of the risks and costs of litigation, or in view of future implementation of the standard. In such cases, the implementer may seek a suitable discount to the royalty.

The number of existing patents changes over time. Where there are patent rights which expire, patent rights which are acquired or divested, or patent rights which are newly registered, the number of patents subject to licensing will change.

d. Value of Individual Patents

Since the value of individual SEPs is inherently different, in calculating an appropriate royalty, sometimes weights are used rather than a simple ownership ratio to reflect the value of individual patents more accurately[81]. In such cases, some argue that patents that are extremely important to the standard should command a higher rate, while patents that are less important should command a lower rate. Others suggest that patents that have been inflated through divisional patent application should command a lower rate.

In cases where the parties involved find it not practical to accurately analyze the value of individual patents, however, the value of individual patents is treated as equal (pro rata)[82].

e. Negotiating History

The negotiation history between the parties is another factor that influences the determination of an appropriate royalty. If there is no difference in the royalty agreed with an implementer who has engaged in negotiations in good faith and that with an implementer who has acted in bad faith, there will be little incentive to negotiate in good faith. From that perspective, one approach is to give a suitable discount to a licensee who concludes a license soon after receiving a license offer, or one who requests a license before an offer is made.

In this way, the length of the negotiating period for an implementer compared to that for other implementers in similar situations may be a factor in determining an appropriate royalty. There is a possibility that an implementer who delays or impedes negotiations will pay a substantially higher royalty.

Likewise, the royalty may become higher after a lawsuit has been initiated, as compared

---

81.In In re Innovatio (U.S., federal district court, 2013), for example, the rights holder's patents were all of moderate to moderate-high importance to the standard, and therefore warranted a higher rate as compared to other patents essential to the standard. In Unwired Planet v. Huawei (UK, high court, 2017), the court allowed both parties to call expert witnesses to weigh the value of each patent. In Apple v. Samsung (Japan, IP high court, 2014), the court took patent weighing into consideration in determining that the contribution of the patent subject to litigation was not large.

82.In addition, one royalty allocation method is based on the number of technologies adopted among contributions at the standard formulation stage, not the number of declared patents. This method can eliminate the influence of non-essential patents.

to a case in which the parties came to an agreement in the negotiations. In license negotiations, a rights holder may offer pre-litigation licensing rates at a discount. This indicates that once litigation starts, what is considered a reasonable royalty may become higher[83].

On the other hand, some argue that because FRAND terms require rights holder to license SEPs to a wide range of parties, it is not suitable to give discounts to parties acquiring licenses early, or to demand high royalties from parties who delayed negotiations or took the rights holder to court.

B. Non-discriminatory Royalties

SEP holders can demand royalties at FRAND terms from implementers, but those royalties have to be non-discriminatory. There are disputes regarding what constitutes non-discriminatory.

1. Concept of Non-Discrimination

Although FRAND licensing terms have to be non-discriminatory, this does not mean that all potential licensees must obtain licenses at the same royalty rate and amount. It is instead considered to mean that similarly situated licensees should not be treated differently[84]. Factors in considering whether licensees are similarly situated include whether the standard technology is used in the same way, the level of the company in the supply chain, and the geographic scope of the licensees' business activities[85][86].

2. Royalties for Different Uses

In an IoT era, ICT is being used in various industries, and some rights holders consequently argue for different royalty rates and amounts for the same standard technology according to the particular use of that technology in the end product.

---

83. In Laser Dynamics v. Quanta (U.S., CAFC 2012), the court recognized that licensing rates in settlement agreements entered into during litigation may be higher than the rate that would have been reached outside of litigation due to the coercive nature of litigation itself.

84. In Unwired Planet v. Huawei (UK, high court, 2017), the court stated that it is discriminatory if the difference in the royalty rates distorts competition between the two licensees in the market. In TCL v. Ericsson (U.S., federal district court, 2017), regardless of whether it generally distorts the development of competition or standards, even if the implementer is alone, the court stated that it is discriminatory if the difference in the royalty rates causes damage.

85. In TCL v. Ericsson (U.S., federal district court, 2017), the court concluded that the following factors could be considered in determining whether two companies are similarly situated: the geographic scope of the companies, the licenses required by the companies, and sales volumes. The court also concluded that the following factors should not be considered in determining whether two companies are similarly situated: overall financial success or risk, brand recognition, the operating systems of their devices, and the existence of retail stores.

86. Courts are divided on whether or not the FRAND rate should be a range. In Microsoft v. Motorola (U.S., federal district court, 2013), the court determined an upper and lower bound of the FRAND range for Motorola's SEP portfolio. On the other hand, in Unwired Planet v. Huawei (UK, high court, 2017), the court determined that each region has only one FRAND royalty rate apiece.

Specifically, in the ICT field, there is a view that it is not discriminatory for a rights holder to apply different royalties for the same standard technology for products that fully utilize the functions of the technology (e.g., high-speed, highcapacity; low latency) and those that only use some of the functions of the technology.

On the other hand, some implementers argue that the same royalty rates and amounts should be applied for the same standard technology regardless of the means by or extent to which it is used.

Specifically, they argue that if different rates and amounts are allowed according to the means of utilization of a technology, it could lead to the value created by downstream inventors being allotted to rights holders, running counter to the "ex ante" principle. In addition, there is one view that where suppliers are granted licenses based on SSPPU, because the application of the suppliers' components is unknown, it can be difficult to apply different royalties depending on the end-product.

C. Other

There are several methods for paying royalties, and different methods will be selected depending on the circumstances.

1. Fixed Rate and Fixed Amount

There is a fixed royalty rate and a fixed royalty amount. A fixed royalty rate is determined as a ratio of the price of the whole product and the price of product components. It is necessary for implementers to know the price of products at all times when the price fluctuates according to market conditions, involving complicated procedures.

In order to reduce such complications, in practice, a method of deciding on a fixed amount of royalties per unit regardless of fluctuations in the price of a product may be used. Although it then becomes relatively simple to collect royalties in such a case, when the price of a royalty-bearing product varies over time, this may result in the royalties on product prices becoming too high or low for implementers.

2. Lump-Sum Payment and Running Royalty Payments

There are lump-sum payments and running royalty payments for paying royalties[87].

For lump-sum payments, there are advantages in being able to avoid the risks of non-payment of royalties and the burden of monitoring whether the technology is

---

87.In Lucent v. Gateway (U.S., CAFC, 2009), the court stated that a running royalty is risky to rights holders because such a royalty is subject to the sales of the implementer, while a lumpsum payment does not require monitoring of sales. On the other hand, the court stated that a lumpsum payment has the benefit of being easy to calculate but may not accurately reflect the value of the patent to the technology.

being used. At the same time, with the royalty fixed and paid before the future sales performance of the implementer's product (the actual usage of the technology in the market) has been established, royalties may in hindsight be too high or too low.

Consequently, where both the rights holder and the implementer seek to conclude a lump-sum royalty agreement, they generally set terms that take into consideration predicted product sales.

For running royalty payments, although it is possible to calculate royalties that reflect the actual usage of the technology, this adds the cost of monitoring to make sure the amount to be paid will increase or decrease appropriately in response to changes in sales.

3. Past Component and Future Component

Royalties paid by those implementing SEPs from the past into the future can be calculated by considering both past and future implementation. In such cases, different formulas are used to calculate past and future royalties. For example, there are cases where the past royalty component has been calculated as a lump sum while the future component is calculated using a fixed-rate running formula.

4. Volume Discounts and Cap (Paid-up)

As an incentive to large-scale implementers, a discount rate may be applied for royalty payments over a certain level, or a ceiling set for royalty payments.

Postscript

Why has the Japan Patent Office engaged with the issue of SEP licensing negotiations? A year ago, it was proposed that JPO look into the introduction of an administrative adjudication system to determine SEP licensing terms. We concluded that a system based on implementer petitions would upset the balance between rights holders and implementers. We were also concerned that introducing such a system would send the wrong message at home and abroad that JPO is dismissive of rights holders' concerns.

How, then, could we address implementers' concern that the smooth introduction of new technologies could well be blocked depending on the way in which SEPs were exercised? Our answer was to provide information that would help implementers without experience in this field to engage in licensing negotiations more effectively and efficiently, forestall disputes, and achieve early dispute resolution.

From fall 2017 through to spring 2018, we sought the views of experts here and abroad to gain a sense of the debates underway around the world. There was no way to absorb such a massive amount of constantly evolving information. We decided to concentrate on setting up the most open process we could manage to garner a broad range of information and opinions, identify the key issues, and present these in a balanced and straightforward manner.

This Guide was compiled by a small team in a limited amount of time, and is consequently far from perfect. Our presentation of both sides of the debate may also be difficult to follow in some places, but it does reflect the heat of the discussion and the lack of convergence over certain points.

That convergence will eventually emerge as technologies and markets continue to evolve and cases of dispute resolution accumulate, while new issues too will inevitably emerge. We look forward to updating this Guide as appropriate with reference to advice from experts here and abroad.

Naoko Munakata
Commissioner

Reference

Japan

- Apple v. Samsung (Japan, IP high court, 2014)
  Case No. 2013 (Ne) 10043
- Imation v. One-Blue (Japan, district court, 2015)
  Case No. 2013 (Wa) 21383
- Softbank v. Kanematsu (Japan, IP high court, 2015)
  Case No. 2015 (Ne) 10069

U.S.

- Apple v. Motorola (U.S., CAFC, 2014)
  Apple, Inc. v. Motorola, Inc., 757 F.3d 1286 (Fed. Cir. 2014), overruled on other grounds by Williamson v. Citrix Online, LLC, 792 F.3d 1339 (Fed. Cir. 2015).
- CSIRO v. Cisco (U.S., CAFC, 2015)
  Commonwealth Scientific and Indus. Research Organization v. Cisco Sys., Inc., 809 F.3d 1295 (Fed. Cir. 2015).
- Cornell University v. Hewlett-Packard (U.S., federal district court, 2009)
  Cornell University v. Hewlett- Packard Co., 609 F.Supp.2d 279 (N.D.N.Y. 2009).
- eBay v. MercExchange (U.S., Supreme Court, 2006)
  eBay Inc. v. MercExchange, LLC, 547 U.S. 388 (2006).

· Ericsson v. D-Link (U.S., CAFC, 2014)

  Ericsson, Inc. v. D-Link Systems, Inc., 773 F.3d 1201 (Fed. Cir. 2014).

· Fujitsu v. Netgear (U.S., CAFC, 2010)

  Fujitsu v. Netgear, 620 F.3d 1321 (Fed. Cir. 2010).

· In re Innovatio (U.S., federal district court, 2013)

  Innovatio IP Ventures, LLC Patent Litigation, No. 11-c-9308, 2013 WL5593609 (Oct. 3, 2013).

· LaserDynamics v. Quanta (U.S., CAFC, 2012)

  LaserDynamics, Inc. v. Quanta Computer, Inc., 694 F.3d 51 (Fed. Cir. 2012).

· Lucent v. Gateway (U.S., CAFC, 2009)

  Lucent Technologies, Inc. v. Gateway, Inc., 580 F.3d 1301 (Fed. Cir. 2009).

· Microsoft v. Motorola (U.S., federal district court, 2012)

  Microsoft Corp. v. Motorola, Inc., 864 F. Supp. 2d 1023 (W.D. Was. 2012).

· Microsoft v. Motorola (U.S., court of appeals for the ninth circuit, 2012)

  Microsoft Corp. v. Motorola, Inc., 696 F.3d 872 (9th Cir. 2012)

· Microsoft v. Motorola (U.S., federal district court, 2013)

  Microsoft Corp. v. Motorola, Inc., No.c-10-1823JLR, 2013 WL 2111217 (W.D. Was. Apr. 25, 2013).

· Quanta v. LG (U.S., Supreme Court, 2008)

  Quanta Computer, Inc. v. LG Elecs., Inc., 553 U.S. 617 (2008).

· Realtek v. LSI (U.S., federal district court, 2013)

  Realtek Semiconductor Corp. v. LSI Corp., 946 F. Supp. 2d 998 (N.D. Cal. 2013).

· ResQNet v. Lansa (U.S., CAFC, 2010)

  ResQNet.com, Inc. v. Lansa, Inc., 594 F.3d 860 (Fed. Cir. 2010).

· TCL v. Ericsson (U.S., federal district court, 2017)

  TCL Comm. Tech Holdings, Ltd v. Ericsson, No.8-14-cv-00341 (C.D. Cal. Dec. 21, 2017).

· Therasense v. Becton (U.S., CAFC, 2011)

  Therasense, Inc. v. Becton, Dickinson and Co., 649 F.3d 1276 (Fed. Cir. 2011) (en banc).

· Virnetx v. Cisco (U.S., CAFC, 2014)

  Virnetx, Inc. v. Cisco Sys., Inc., 767 F.3d 1308 (Fed. Cir. 2014).

EU

· Huawei v. ZTE (EU, CJEU, 2015)

  Case C-170/13, Huawei Technologies Co. Ltd v ZTE Corp., ZTE Deutschland GmbH [2015] CJEU

· Motorola v. Apple (EU, EC, 2014)

  European Commission, DG Competition, Decision of 29 April 2014, C(2014) 2892 final, Motorola Mobility Inc.

· NTT DoCoMo v. HTC (Germany, district court, 2016)

LG Mannheim, Case 7 O 66/15, Order of 29 January 2016

· Philips v. Archos (Germany, district court, 2016)

LG Mannheim, Case 7 O 19/16, Order of 17 November 2016

· Samsung v. Apple (EU, EC, 2014)

European Commission, DG Competition, Commitment Decision of 29 April 2014, C(2014) 2891 final, Samsung Electronics Co., Ltd., et. Al.

· Sisvel v. Haier (Germany, high court, 2016)

OLG Düsseldorf, Case I-15 U 66/15, Order of 17 November 2016

· St. Lawrence v. Deutsche Telekom and HTC (Germany, district court, 2015)

LG Mannheim, Case 2 O 106/14, Order of 27 November 2015

· St. Lawrence v. Vodafone and HTC (Germany, district court, 2016)

LG Düsseldorf, Case 4a O 73/14, Order of 31 March 2016

· Unwired Planet v. Huawei (UK, high court, 2017)

Unwired Planet v. Huawei ([2017] EWHC 711 (Pat), 5 Apr. 2017)

China

· Huawei v. Samsung (CN, intermediate court, 2018)

Case No. 816 of 2016

Other

· "Benefits of Arbitration for Commercial Disputes", American Bar Association

https://www.americanbar.org/content/dam/aba/events/dispute_resolution/committees/ arbitration/arbitrationguide.authcheckdam.pdf

· European communication

Communication from the Commission to the European Parliament, the Council and the European Economic and Social Committee: Setting out the EU approach to Standard Essential Patents

· IEEE-SA Standards Board Bylaws (2015)

http://standards.ieee.org/develop/policies/bylaws/approved-changes.pdf

· Makan Delrahim, Assistant Attorney General, Antitrust Division, U.S. Department of Justice, "Take it to the Limit: Respecting Innovation Incentives in the Application of Antitrust Law," Remarks as prepared for delivery at USC Gould School of Law – Application of Competition Policy to Technology and IP Licensing (Nov. 10, 2017) ("Innovation Incentives Speech") https://www.justice.gov/opa/speech/file/1010746/download

· New York Convention

http://www.newyorkconvention.org/

· The Japan Fair Trade Commission the "Guidelines for Use of Intellectual Property under the

Antimonopoly Act"

https://www.jftc.go.jp/en/legislation_gls/imonopoly_guidelines_files/IPGL_Frand.pdf

・U.S. Dep't of Justice and Federal Trade Commission, Antitrust Guidelines (2017)

U.S. Dep't of Justice and Federal Trade Commission, Antitrust Guidelines for the Licensing of Intellectual Property (Jan. 12, 2017)

・U.S. Dep't of Justice and U.S. Patent and Trademark Office, Policy Statement (2013)

U.S. Dep't of Justice and U.S. Patent and Trademark Office, Policy Statement on Remedies for Standard-Essential Patents Subject to Voluntary FRAND Commitments (Jan. 8, 2013)

Bibliography

Books

Albors-Llorens, A., *EC Competition Law and policy* (Willan, 2002)

Anderman, S.D, *EC Competition Law and Intellectual Property Rights: The Regulation of Innovation* (Oxford University Press, 1998)

Anderman, S.D. and Kallaugher, J., *Technology Transfer and the New EU Competition Rules* (Oxford University Press, 2009)

Asabane, S., *Strategy of Competition and Corporation* (Yuuhikaku,1994)

Atsuya, J., *Dokusenkinshi hou nyuumon [Introduction of Antimonopoly Act]*(7thedn., Nihonkeizaishinbun, 2012)

Bergh, R.J.V. den, & P.D.Camesasca, *European Competition Law and Economics: A Comparative Perspective* (2ndedn., Sweet & Maxwell, 2006)

Brandenburger, A.M., & B.J. Nalebuff, *Co-opetition* (Currency Doubleday, 1996)

Coskeran, T., *Economics, a complete introduction* (Hodder Education, 2012)

Cucinotta, A., R. Pardolesi, , & R.J.V. den Bergh (eds), *Post-Chicago Developments in Antitrust Law* (Edward Elgar Publishing, 2003)

Davis, J., *Intellectual Property Law* (4thedn., Oxford University Press, 2008)

Ezrachi, A., *EU Competition Law, an analytical guide to the leading cases* (6thedn., Hart Publishing, 2018)

Ezrachi. A.(ed.), *Article 82 EC: Reflections on its Recent Evolution* (Hart Publishing, 2009)

Fuchikawa, K., "Beikoku hantorasuto hou ni okeru kaitejigyousha kan no kyoudoukoui kisei [Analysis of regulation on purchaser's cartel under US antitrust law]", CPRC Discussion Paper Series (2012), available at:

http://www.jftc.go.jp/cprc/discussionpapers/h23/cpdp_55_j_abstract.files/
CPDP-55-J.pdf

Fujino, J., *Tokkyo to Gijutsu Hyoujun [Patents and Technological Standard]* (Hassakusha, 1998)

Gillespie, A., *Foundations of Economics,*(2ⁿᵈedn., Oxford University Press, 2011)

Goto, A. & S. Nagaoka, (ed.), *Chitekizaisan seido to innovation [IP rights system and Innovation]* (Tokyo daigaku shuppankai, 2003)

Goto, A., & A. Nagata, *NISTEP Report :Innovation no senyuukanousei to gijutsukikai [NISTEP Report: Appropriability of Innovation and Technological Opportunity]* (NISTEP, 1997)

Goto, A., & A. Yamada, (ed.), *IT kakumei to kyousou seisaku [IT revolution and competition policy]* (Touyou keizai shinpousha, 2001)

Greenhalgh, C., & M. Rogers, *Innovation, Intellectual Property, and Economic Growth* (Princeton University Press, 2010)

Ghidini,G., *Intelecutal Property and Competition Law, The Innovation Nexus,* (Edward Elgar Publishing, 2006)

Guellec, D., and B.van Pottelsberghe, *The economics of the European Patent System* (Oxford University Press, 2007)

Hatzopoulos, V., "Refusal to deal" in Amato, G.,& C.D. Ehlermann (eds), *EC Competition Law* (Hart Publishing, 2007)

Hawkins, E.R., R. Mansell, & J. Skea, (eds.)., *Standards, Innovation and Competitiveness : The Politics and Economics of Standards in Natural and Technical Environments* (Edward Elgar Publishing,1995)

Hirooka, M., *Gijutu kakushin to keizai hatten [Technology progress and economic growth]* (Nihon keizai shinbunsha, 2003)

Hitotsubashi daigaku kenkyuu center (ed.), *Innovation Management nyuumon [Introduction of innovation management]* (Nihonkeizai shinbun sha, 2001)

Imamura,N., *Dokusenkinshi hou nyuumon [Introduction of Anti-Monopoly Act]* (Yuuhikaku, 1993)

Ishigaki, H., & T. Igarashi, "Suichoku kongougata kigyou ketsugou kisei no hougaku keizaigaku teki kanngaekata ni kansuru chousa [Legal/economic analysis on regulation of vertical/mixed mergers]" ,Competition Policy Research Centre Collaborative Report (2004), available at:
https://www.jftc.go.jp/cprc/reports/index.files/cr0404.pdf

Itou, M., *Micro keizaigaku [Micro Economics]* (Nihonhyouronsha, 1993)

Iwata, K., *Zeminar Micro keizaigaku nyuumon [Seminar: Introduction of Micro Economics]* (Nihonkeizai-shinbunsha, 1993)

Jacob, R., *IP and Other Things: A Collection of Essays and Speeches* (Hart Publishing Ltd, 2015)

Kanai, T., N. Kawahama, & F. Sensui, *Dokusenkinshi hou [Antimonopoly Act]*, (6th edn., Shouji Houmu, 2018)

Korah, V., *Intellectual Property Rights and the EC Competition Rules* (Hart Publishing, 2006)

Miyata, Y., *America no innovation seisaku [American innovation policy]* (Shouwado, 2011)

Mukai. N, Kyousouhou ni okeru kyousei raisensutou no jitsumu [Compulsory license under Anti-monopoly Act] (Chuoukeizaisha, 2010)

Negishi, T., & M. Funada, *Dokusenkinshi hou gaisetsu [Abstract of Antimonopoly Act]*, (Yuuhikaku, 2000)

Nordhaus, W.D., *Invention, Growth and Welfare* (MIT Press, 1969)

Okuno, M., *Micro keizaigaku nyuumon [Introduction of Micro Economics]* (2nd edn., Nihonkeizai-shinbunsha, 1990)

Pace, L.F. (ed.), *European Competition Law, The impact of the Commission's Guidance on Article 102* (Edward Elgar Publishing, 2011)

Pitofsky, R. (ed.), *How the Chicago school overshot the mark : The effect of conservative economic analysis on U.S. Anti-trust* (Oxford University Press, 2008)

Rosgger, G., *The Economics of Production and Innovation* (2nd edn., Pregamon Press, 1986)

Yamada, H., *Gijutsu kyousou to sekai hyoujun [Techonolgy competition and global standard]* (NTT Shuppan, 1999)

Yorida, T., *Network Economics* (Nihon Hyouronsha, 2001)

Sanekata, K., *Dokusenkinshi hou [Anti-monopoly Act]* (4th edn., Yuuhikaku, 1998)

Scotcmer, S., *Innovation and Incentives* (MIT Press, 2004)

Scherer, F.M., *Competition Policy, Domestic and International* (Edward Elgar Publishing, 2000)

Shapiro, C., & H.R. Varian, *Information Rules* (Harvard Business School Press, 1998)

Shavell, S., *Foundations of Economic Analysis of Law* (Belknap Press of Harvard, 2004)

Shintaku,J., Y. Kyoi, & K. Sibata (ed.), *De facto standard no honshitsu [The essence of de facto standard]* (Yuuhikaku, 2000)

Shiraishi, D., *Gijutsu to kyousou no houtekikouzou [Legal structure of technology and competition]* (Yuhikaku, 1994)

Anderman, S., & A. Ezrachi (eds.), *Intellectual Property and Competition Law: New Frontiers* (Oxford University Press, 2011)

Schumpeter, J.A., *Capitalis, Socialism and Democracy* (Harper, 1942)

Scherer, F.M., *Innovation and Growth: Schumpeterian Perspectives* (MIT Press, 1984)

Takigawa, T., *High-tech sangyou no chitekizaisannken to dokukinnhou [Intellectual Property Rights and Antimonopoly Act in IT market],* (Tsushousangyou Chousakai, 2000)

Takigawa, T., *Nichibei EU no dokukinhou to kyousou seisaku [Competition law in Japan, US and EU and competition policy* (3rd edn., Seirinshoin, 2006)

Tamura, Y., *Chiteki zaisann hou [Intellectual Property Law]*, (2ndedn., Yuhikaku, 2000)

Tamura, Y., *Shijyou, Jiyuu, Chitekizaisan [Market, freedom and IP rights]* (Yuuhikaku, 2004)

Tanaka, T., Y. Yazaki, & R. Murakami, "Network gaibusei no keizai bunseki [Economic Analysis of Network Externality]" ,Competition Policy Research Centre Collaborative Report (2003), available at:
https://www.jftc.go.jp/cprc/reports/index.files/cr0103.pdf

Tsuchii, Y., *Gijutsu hyoujun to kyousou [Technological Standard and Competition]*, (Nihonkeizai Hyouronsha, 2001)

Wakui, M., *Gijutsu hyoujun wo meguru hou sissutemu [Law system regarding technological standards]* (Kobundo, 2010)

Watanabe, A., "Yuetsuteki chi no ranyoukisei no houteki ichiduke to kongo no kisei no arikata [The legal status of abuse of bargaining power and its future reform]" in Kyoto University Graduate School of Public Policy (eds),*2010 Research Paper Collection* (Kyoto University, 2010)

Articles

Albors-Llorens, A. "Refusal to deal and objective justification in EC Competition Law" (2006) 65 Cambridge Law Journal 24

Albors-Llorens, A., "The essential facilities doctrine in EC Competition law" (1999) 58 Cambridge Law Journal 490

Albors-Llorens, A. "The role of objective justification and efficiencies in the application of Article 82 EC" (2007) 48Cambridge Law Journal 17

Andreangeli, A., "Case note on T-201/04, Microsoft v Commission, judgment of 17 September 2007" (2008) 44(3) Common Market Law Review 863

Andreangeli, A., "Interoperability as an essential facility in the Microsoft case—encouraging competition or stifling innovation?" (2009) 34(4) European Law Review 584

Anton, J.J. & Yao, D.A, Standard Setting Consortia, "Antitrust, and High-Technology Industries" (1995) 64 Antitrust L.J. 247

Bishop, W., "Essential Facilities: The Rising Tide" (1998) 4 European Competition Law Review 183

Cascón, C., "La problemática de las patentes indispensables en estándares técnicos y la eficacia de los compromisos de licencia en términos FRAND [The problem of technical standards essential patents and the effectiveness of FRAND license commitments]" (2016) 3 REVISTA ELECTRÓNLOA DE DIREITO 1

Cohen, E., & D. Levinthal, "Innovation and learning: the two faces of R&D" (1989) 99 Economic Journal 569

Farrell, J., & G. Saloner, " Installed Base and Compatibility, and Innovation" (1986) 16 Rand Journal of Economics 70

Fox, E.M., "Microsoft (EC) and Duty to Deal : Exceptionality and the Transatlantic Divide" (2008) 4 Competition Policy International 25

Fujiwara,J., "Oushu ni okeru essenshal facility ron no keisju [The essential facilities doctrine in the Europe]- part 2" , (2001) 74-3 Hougaku-kenkyu 37

Goikoetxea, I.M., *Why the Magill criteria should have been reviewed in IMS Health and the effectiveness of compulsory licence*" (2019) 40 (1) European Competition Law Review 24

Goikoetxea, I.M., "Huawei v ZTE should have been treated as a refusal to contract — to grant SEP licences — and not as a new category of abuse" (2019) 40(2) European Competition Law Review 67

Greenhalgh,C., & M. Rogers, "The value of innovation : the interaction of competition, R&D and IP" (2004) 35 Research Policy 562

Kawahama, N., "Gijustsu hyoujun to dokusenkinshi hou [Technological standard and antimonopoly act]" (2000) 146-3/4 Hougakuronsou 115

Hagiwara, Y., "Gijutsukakushin to senyuukanousei [Technological Innovation and Appropriability]" (2008) 1 For Study of Economics/Business Administration 19

Hildebrand, D., "The European School in EC Competition Law" (2002) 25 World Competition 3

Katz, M.L., & C. Shapiro, "Network Externalities, Competition, and Compatibility", (1985) 75 American Economic Review 424

Kawahama, N., "Shijyou chitsujyohou to shitenno dokkinhou [AMA as Market Principle Law] (1)", (2008) 139-3 Mishouhou-zasshi 265

Klemperer, P., "How broad should the scope of patents be?" (1990) 23 Rand Journal of Economics 113

Lang, J.T., "Competition Law and Regulation Law from an EC Perspectives", (2000) 23 Fordham International Law Journal, 116

Lang, J.T., "Defining Legitimate Competition: Company's Duties to Supply Competition and Access to Essential Facilities", (1994) 18 Fordham International Law Journal, 437

Lemley, M.A., & D. McGowan, "Legal Implications of Network Economic Effects", (1998) 86 California Law Review 479

Malshe, D., "Essential Facilities: de facto; de jure" (2019) 40 (3)European Competition Law Review 124

Mansfield, E., "Patents and innovation: an empirical study", (1986) 32 Management Science 173

Nordhaus, W. D., "The optimum life of a patent: Reply" (1972) 62 American Economic Review 428

Pardolesi, R., & A. Renda, "The European Commission's case against Microsoft: Kill Bill?" (2004) 27 World Competition 513

Peralta, E.O., "Una vuelta a la aplicacion de la doctrina de las facilidades esenciales (essential facilities) a la propiedad intelectual e industrial [A return to the application of the doctrine of essential facilities (essential facilities) to intellectual and industrial property]" (2016) 19 REVISTA DE DERECHO DE LA COMPETENCIA Y LA DISTRIBUOIÓN 14

Petit, N., "Injunctions for Frand-Pledged SEPs: The Quest for an Appropriate Test of Abuse Under Article 102 TFEU" , (2013) 9(3) EUROPEAN COMPETITION JOURNAL 677

Petit, N., "EU Competition Law Analysis of FRAND Disputes" , in (Contreras ed., 2017) THE CAMBRIDGE HANDBOOK TECHNOLOGICAL STANDARDIZATION LAW: COMPETIION, ANTITRUST, AND PATENTS 29

Ridyard, D., "Essential Facilities and the Obligation to Supply Competitors under UK and EC Competition Law" , (1996) European Competition Law Review, 438

Ridyard, D., "Compulsory Access under EC Competition Law — A New Doctrine of "Convenient Facilities" and the Case for Price Regulation" (2004) 25 European Competition Law Review 669

Ritter, C., "Refusal to Deal and Essential Facilities: Does Intellectual Property Require Special Deference compared to Tangible Property?" (2005) 3 World Competition: Law and Economics Review 281

Shapiro, C., "Systems Competition and Network Effects" (1994) 8 Journal of Economic Perspectives 93

Tanaka, S., "Gijutsuchisiki no seishitsu to chitekizaisan seido, kyousou sisaku noyakuwari [Nature of Technological Knowledge and the Role of Intellectual Property Rights System/Competition Policy]" , (2003) 54 Foreign Study 17

Werra J.D., "Les licences FRAND: Chance ou risque pour l' harmonisation globale du droit des contrats de licence de brevets? [FRAND licenses: Chance or risk for the global harmonization of patent licensing contract law?]" , (2019) 2 Sic! 77

Yanagawa,T., "Torihikihiyou keizaigaku to yuuetsuteki chii no ranyou [Transaction cost economy and abuse of bargaining power]" (2008) 697 Kouseitorihiki 8

Index

[Author]

Prof. Seiya S. Takeuchi (Esq.)

Japan Patent Attorney

Graduate School of Innovation and Technology Management, Yamaguchi University
(National University of Yamaguchi)

B.A. in Economics, Keio University 【Japan】(1996)

LL.B, Keio University 【Japan】(1998)

LL.M, Graduate School of Law, Chuo University 【Japan】(2003)

Research LL.M, Graduate Research Law Program, Law School, University of Edinburgh
【UK】(2012-13)

Graduate Presessional Program, University of Oxford 【UK】(2013)

Academic Visitor Scholar, Faculty of Law, University of Oxford 【UK】(2016-2020)

Academic Visitor Scholar, Faculty of Law, University College London 【UK】(2019)

IP Law Specialist, Law and IP Headquarters, Mitsubishi Electric Corporation 【Japan】
(1998-2003)

Deputy-Senior Manager Patent Attorney, IP Law Department, IBM Japan Corporation
【Japan】(2003-2015)

Professor, Graduate School of Innovation and Technology Management, Yamaguchi
University 【Japan】(2015- Present)

Registered Arbitrator/Mediator, IP Dispute Resolution Centre, WIPO【UN】(2019-
Present)

Vice President of Chugoku District, Japan Patent Attorney Association 【Japan】(2020-
Present)

◎本書スタッフ

マネージャー：大塚 浩昭

編集長：石井 沙知

表紙デザイン：tplot.inc 中沢 岳志

技術開発・システム支援：インプレスR&D NextPublishingセンター

●本書の内容についてのお問い合わせ先

近代科学社Digital　メール窓口

kdd-info@kindaikagaku.co.jp

件名に「『本書名』問い合わせ係」と明記してお送りください。

電話やFAX、郵便でのご質問にはお答えできません。返信までには、しばらくお時間をい
ただく場合があります。なお、本書の範囲を超えるご質問にはお答えしかねますので、あ
らかじめご了承ください。

Analysis of Enforcement of Intellectual Property Rights Related to Standard Technology in East Asia and Europe

2021年2月26日　初版発行Ver.1.0

著　者　竹内 誠也
発行人　井芹 昌信
発　行　近代科学社Digital
販　売　株式会社近代科学社
　　　　〒162-0843
　　　　東京都新宿区市谷田町2-7-15
　　　　https://www.kindaikagaku.co.jp

印刷・製本　京葉流通倉庫株式会社
Printed in Japan

ISBN978-4-7649-6016-9

近代科学社 Digital は、株式会社近代科学社が推進する21世紀型の理工系出版レーベルです。デジタルパワーを積極活用することで、オンデマンド型のスピーディで持続可能な出版モデルを提案します。

近代科学社Digitalは株式会社インプレスR&Dのデジタルファースト出版プラットフォーム"NextPublishing"との協業で実現しています。